10 <u>Very Recent</u>
ACTUAL, OFFICIAL
LSAT PREPTESTS

Official LSAT PrepTests 61–70

Published by
Cambridge LSAT
225 W. Verdugo Ave., #302
Burbank, CA 91502

Author: Morley Tatro

Manufactured in the United States
November 2013

ISBN-10: 0-615-91468-3
ISBN-13: 978-0-615-91468-8

Official LSAT content delivered instantly to your computer!

www.cambridgelsat.com

Full-Length Tests   **Individual Sections**   **Drilling Problem Sets**   **Prep Books**   **Explanations**   **Bundles**

If you're preparing for the LSAT (Law School Admission Test), chances are you understand the importance of this crucial admission test. In order to perform at your highest potential, quality preparation is critical. With so many prep courses and guides on the market, it's easy to become confused. The key to preparation is consistent and effective use of real LSAT questions. Until recently, it has been very difficult to acquire real LSAT questions in various groupings. Short of shelling out the money for an expensive prep course, you would have to go through the time-consuming process of breaking up PrepTests into question/game/passage types. Cambridge LSAT has the answer. We have done all that for you, so that you can allocate your time effectively. In addition to being broken down by type, our question/game/passage groupings are each presented in order of increasing difficulty, so that you can start with the most manageable content and progress through the most difficult material the LSAT has to offer. The site also features a number of useful free resources, including a test tracking spreadsheet, a Logic Games tracker, advice, an LSAT FAQ, tutor listings, Logic Games practice, prep book excerpts/recommendations, and June 2007 LSAT explanations. Stop by today and download the materials you need.

Why Cambridge LSAT?
o   You can print clean copies when needed to redo problems
o   No need to wait for books in the mail or go to the bookstore
o   Eliminates the cost of shipping
o   No need to tear out pages should you need to separate particular problems into groups
o   Gives you immediate access to real test content
o   You can purchase questions in whatever grouping fits your study plan
o   You can acquire tests/questions that are hard to find and/or out-of-print

Have a question, comment, or concern? E-mail us at info@cambridgelsat.com.

Available at www.cambridgelsat.com/bookstore/

LSAT Logic Games Drilling Workbooks, Volumes 1, 2, and 3

LSAT Logical Reasoning Drilling Workbooks, Volumes 1, 2, and 3

LSAT Reading Comprehension Drilling Workbooks, Volumes 1, 2, and 3

10 Actual, Official LSAT PrepTests (Out-of-Print, Recent, and More Recent)

LSAT Endurance Training, Volumes 1, 2, and Extreme Edition

LSAT Logic Games Repetition Workbooks, Volumes 1, 2, and 3

LSAT Logic Games Solutions Manual

The Big Fat Genius Guide to LSAT Logic Games

LSAT Logical Reasoning Strategy Guide Workbook

Ultimate LSAT Prep Package

TABLE OF CONTENTS

INTRODUCTION

About the LSAT

The LSAT, or Law School Admission Test, is a half-day standardized test which is used to compare candidates for admission to most law schools in the United States and Canada. The test consists of four scored multiple-choice sections, one unscored multiple-choice section, and one unscored Writing Sample. The test is administered four times each year, once in each of four months: February, June, September or October, and December. As of 2001, the February administrations have been undisclosed, which means that they are not released to the test takers, nor are they released as PrepTests.

The following table illustrates the structure of the test:

Section Type	Time	Scored?	Questions
Logical Reasoning	35 minutes	Yes	24–26
Logical Reasoning	35 minutes	Yes	24–26
Logic Games (Analytical Reasoning)	35 minutes	Yes	22–24
Reading Comprehension	35 minutes	Yes	26–28
Experimental (one of the above types)	35 minutes	No	22–28
Writing Sample	35 minutes	No	NA

Keep in mind that, with the exception of the Writing Sample, which is always given as the sixth section, these sections can appear in any order. In previous years, the experimental section was consistently among the first three sections; however, recent test administrations have broken with this tradition. The first three sections are completed consecutively without any breaks. There is a 10 to 15 minute break in between the third and fourth sections. The fourth and fifth sections are completed consecutively, and then the test booklets are collected. Once you have completed the Writing Sample, the test day is over.

LSAT PrepTests

In June of 1991, the modern format of the LSAT was unveiled and administered for the first time. LSAT PrepTests are previously-administered actual LSATs dating from that initial administration which have been released for the purpose of preparation. Including the three February tests in LSAC's The Official LSAT SuperPrep, there are over 70 available LSAT PrepTests. With so much official content available, there's no compelling reason to practice with anything but real questions. This book contains PrepTests numbered 61 through 70, each in its entirety. These tests were administered from October of 2010 through October of 2013. With the exception of PrepTest 18, the tests are numbered in the order in which they were administered. For a complete list of available PrepTests and their respective administration dates, visit **www.cambridgelsat.com/ resources/data/preptest-numbers-dates/**. LSAC does not release the unscored experimental sections; the questions are subsequently used on scored sections.

INTRODUCTION

Thus, each LSAT PrepTest contains four multiple-choice sections.

Logical Reasoning

Each LSAT features two scored Logical Reasoning sections, each of which contains between 24 and 26 questions. Logical Reasoning questions ask you to critically dissect arguments and fact sets and make inferences from the statements, collectively referred to as the stimulus. Stimuli with argumentation can be followed by any one of the following question types: Main Conclusion, Flaw, Parallel (Reasoning), Parallel (Flaw), Necessary Assumption, Sufficient Assumption, Strengthen, Weaken, Evaluate, Principle (Identify), Principle (Apply), etc. Stimuli without argumentation, typically presented as factual information, tend to be followed by one of the following question types: Must Be True, Most Strongly Supported, Paradox, etc. A thorough understanding of formal logic principles, especially sufficient and necessary conditions, is helpful in answering the most difficult Logical Reasoning questions.

Logic Games (Analytical Reasoning)

The Logic Games, or Analytical Reasoning section, is typically the most intimidating section for people starting out with their preparation. For most, taking a timed Logic Games section without any prior prep work in this area results in incomplete and inaccurate performance. LSAT Logic Games test your ability to deductively examine a framework of relationships and determine what must be true, what could be true, what is not necessarily true, and what cannot be true. Each Analytical Reasoning section consists of exactly four games, or puzzles, and each game is followed by between five and eight questions. Logic Games tend to hinge on at least one of three recurring themes: ordering, grouping, and assignment.

Reading Comprehension

The Reading Comprehension section of the test is generally the most familiar of the three scored section types. Consequently, it can be the most difficult of the three section types in which to make gains. Each Reading Comprehension section features four passages, each followed by between five and eight questions. Since the June 2007 administration (available as a free PrepTest at **www.lsac.org**), every Reading Comprehension section has featured one set of comparative passages in place of one of the single passages. The questions test your command of both global ideas and fine details presented in the passages. Reading Comprehension questions routinely inquire about authors' views, outside views, main points, definitions, passage structures, argumentative functions, and general inferences.

The Experimental Section

LSAC uses a process called equating to ensure that the same score across different test administrations means the same thing. In other words, a 160 on one test should indicate the same level of performance as a 160 on another test. In order to equate the tests, LSAC includes an unscored experimental section with each administration. Multiple experimental sections are used during each administration so that LSAC can pretest a lot of questions. Prior to ever appearing on a scored section of an LSAT, each individual question has undergone extensive testing. In this way, LSAC can control the difficulty levels of the individual scored sections to a high degree of accuracy. The experimental section is always one of the three multiple-choice section types (Logical Reasoning, Logic Games, or Reading Comprehension). There is little use in trying to figure out which section is experimental, and attempting to do so could have a detrimental effect on your score.

The Writing Sample

Since most law school exams involve writing under timed pressure, the LSAT includes a timed Writing Sample, administered as the sixth section of the test. It is unscored. However, each law school to which you apply will receive a copy of your Writing Sample. Thus, it is important that you at least exert some effort in framing an appropriate argument for the topic at hand. The writing prompt is given in the form of a decision prompt. A scenario will be presented, followed by two distinct courses of action. Your job is to persuasively argue one of the two choices. There is no "right" or "wrong" answer; each side will have both positives and negatives. Make sure to write legibly, and back up your position clearly and concisely.

Timed Practice

The time constraints significantly contribute to the LSAT's overall difficulty, and as such, it is important to include regular timed practice in your prep regimen as the date of your scheduled exam approaches. This book is designed so that you can practice under timed conditions with some of the most recent LSAT PrepTests. You can use this book to take either individual sections of tests or full-length, timed tests. Visit **www.cambridgelsat.com/resources/spreadsheets/ test-tracking-spreadsheet/** to pick up a free copy of our test tracking spreadsheet. You can use it to score all ten PrepTests in this book, and it will help you identify particular areas to focus on in your subsequent prep work. If you need to print additional answer sheets, visit **www.cambridgelsat.com/resources/free-downloads/answer-sheets-etc/**.

The Fundamentals

While timed practice is necessary, it is generally not sufficient to reach your maximum potential on the exam. Taking test after test without learning and integrating effective problem-solving strategies is akin to taking algebra tests before learning proper addition, subtraction, multiplication, and division techniques. The logical thinking tested by the LSAT is foreign to the majority of beginning students and it takes time, practice, and patience to assimilate. To master the concepts routinely tested by the LSAT, we recommend that you also purchase at least one reputable strategy guide and problem sets for drilling the different question types. Our website features both downloadable and paperback products which address these critical prep components. Should you have any questions regarding recommended materials, send an e-mail to **info@cambridgelsat.com**.

PREPTEST 61
OCTOBER 2010
FORM 0LSN86

SECTION I

Time—35 minutes

27 Questions

Directions: Each set of questions in this section is based on a single passage or a pair of passages. The questions are to be answered on the basis of what is <u>stated</u> or <u>implied</u> in the passage or pair of passages. For some of the questions, more than one of the choices could conceivably answer the question. However, you are to choose the <u>best</u> answer; that is, the response that most accurately and completely answers the question, and blacken the corresponding space on your answer sheet.

The Universal Declaration of Human Rights (UDHR), approved by the United Nations General Assembly in 1948, was the first international treaty to expressly affirm universal respect for human rights.

(5) Prior to 1948 no truly international standard of humanitarian beliefs existed. Although Article 1 of the 1945 UN Charter had been written with the express purpose of obligating the UN to "encourage respect for human rights and for fundamental

(10) freedoms for all without distinction as to race, sex, language, or religion," there were members of delegations from various small countries and representatives of several nongovernmental organizations who felt that the language of Article 1

(15) was not strong enough, and that the Charter as a whole did not go far enough in its efforts to guarantee basic human rights. This group lobbied vigorously to strengthen the Charter's human rights provisions and proposed that member states be

(20) required "to take separate and joint action and to co-operate with the organization for the promotion of human rights." This would have implied an obligation for member states to act on human rights issues. Ultimately, this proposal and others like it were not

(25) adopted; instead, the UDHR was commissioned and drafted.

The original mandate for producing the document was given to the UN Commission on Human Rights in February 1946. Between that time and the General

(30) Assembly's final approval of the document, the UDHR passed through an elaborate eight-stage drafting process in which it made its way through almost every level of the UN hierarchy. The articles were debated at each stage, and all 30 articles were

(35) argued passionately by delegates representing diverse ideologies, traditions, and cultures. The document as it was finally approved set forth the essential principles of freedom and equality for everyone— regardless of sex, race, color, language, religion,

(40) political or other opinion, national or social origin, property, birth or other status. It also asserted a number of fundamental human rights, including among others the right to work, the right to rest and leisure, and the right to education.

(45) While the UDHR is in many ways a progressive document, it also has weaknesses, the most regrettable of which is its nonbinding legal status. For all its strong language and high ideals, the UDHR remains a resolution of a purely programmatic nature.

(50) Nevertheless, the document has led, even if belatedly, to the creation of legally binding human rights conventions, and it clearly deserves recognition as an international standard-setting piece of work, as a set of aspirations to which UN member states are

(55) intended to strive, and as a call to arms in the name of humanity, justice, and freedom.

1. By referring to the Universal Declaration of Human Rights as "purely programmatic" (line 49) in nature, the author most likely intends to emphasize

(A) the likelihood that the document will inspire innovative government programs designed to safeguard human rights

(B) the ability of the document's drafters to translate abstract ideals into concrete standards

(C) the compromises that went into producing a version of the document that would garner the approval of all relevant parties

(D) the fact that the guidelines established by the document are ultimately unenforceable

(E) the frustration experienced by the document's drafters at stubborn resistance from within the UN hierarchy

2. The author most probably quotes directly from both the UN Charter (lines 8–11) and the proposal mentioned in lines 20–22 for which one of the following reasons?

(A) to contrast the different definitions of human rights in the two documents

(B) to compare the strength of the human rights language in the two documents

(C) to identify a bureaucratic vocabulary that is common to the two documents

(D) to highlight what the author believes to be the most important point in each document

(E) to call attention to a significant difference in the prose styles of the two documents

3. The author's stance toward the Universal Declaration of Human Rights can best be described as

(A) unbridled enthusiasm

(B) qualified approval

(C) absolute neutrality

(D) reluctant rejection

(E) strong hostility

GO ON TO THE NEXT PAGE.

4. According to the passage, each of the following is true of the Universal Declaration of Human Rights EXCEPT:

(A) It asserts a right to rest and leisure.
(B) It was drafted after the UN Charter was drafted.
(C) The UN Commission on Human Rights was charged with producing it.
(D) It has had no practical consequences.
(E) It was the first international treaty to explicitly affirm universal respect for human rights.

5. The author would be most likely to agree with which one of the following statements?

(A) The human rights language contained in Article 1 of the UN Charter is so ambiguous as to be almost wholly ineffectual.
(B) The weaknesses of the Universal Declaration of Human Rights generally outweigh the strengths of the document.
(C) It was relatively easy for the drafters of the Universal Declaration of Human Rights to reach a consensus concerning the contents of the document.
(D) The drafters of the Universal Declaration of Human Rights omitted important rights that should be included in a truly comprehensive list of basic human rights.
(E) The Universal Declaration of Human Rights would be truer to the intentions of its staunchest proponents if UN member countries were required by law to abide by its provisions.

6. Suppose that a group of independent journalists has uncovered evidence of human rights abuses being perpetrated by a security agency of a UN member state upon a group of political dissidents. Which one of the following approaches to the situation would most likely be advocated by present-day delegates who share the views of the delegates and representatives mentioned in lines 11–14?

(A) The UN General Assembly authenticates the evidence and then insists upon prompt remedial action on the part of the government of the member state.
(B) The UN General Assembly stipulates that any proposed response must be unanimously accepted by member states before it can be implemented.
(C) The UN issues a report critical of the actions of the member state in question and calls for a censure vote in the General Assembly.
(D) The situation is regarded by the UN as an internal matter that is best left to the discretion of the government of the member state.
(E) The situation is investigated further by nongovernmental humanitarian organizations that promise to disclose their findings to the public via the international media.

GO ON TO THE NEXT PAGE.

It is commonly assumed that even if some forgeries have aesthetic merit, no forgery has as much as an original by the imitated artist would. Yet even the most prominent art specialists can be duped by a
(5) talented artist turned forger into mistaking an almost perfect forgery for an original. For instance, artist Han van Meegeren's *The Disciples at Emmaus* (1937)—painted under the forged signature of the acclaimed Dutch master Jan Vermeer (1632–1675)—
(10) attracted lavish praise from experts as one of Vermeer's finest works. The painting hung in a Rotterdam museum until 1945, when, to the great embarrassment of the critics, van Meegeren revealed its origin. Astonishingly, there was at least one highly
(15) reputed critic who persisted in believing it to be a Vermeer even after van Meegeren's confession.

Given the experts' initial enthusiasm, some philosophers argue that van Meegeren's painting must have possessed aesthetic characteristics that, in a
(20) Vermeer original, would have justified the critics' plaudits. Van Meegeren's *Emmaus* thus raises difficult questions regarding the status of superbly executed forgeries. Is a forgery inherently inferior as art? How are we justified, if indeed we are, in revising
(25) downwards our critical assessment of a work unmasked as a forgery? Philosopher of art Alfred Lessing proposes convincing answers to these questions.

A forged work is indeed inferior as art, Lessing
(30) argues, but not because of a shortfall in aesthetic qualities strictly defined, that is to say, in the qualities perceptible on the picture's surface. For example, in its composition, its technique, and its brilliant use of color, van Meegeren's work is flawless, even
(35) beautiful. Lessing argues instead that the deficiency lies in what might be called the painting's intangible qualities. All art, explains Lessing, involves technique, but not all art involves origination of a new vision, and originality of vision is one of the
(40) fundamental qualities by which artistic, as opposed to purely aesthetic, accomplishment is measured. Thus Vermeer is acclaimed for having inaugurated, in the seventeenth century, a new way of seeing, and for pioneering techniques for embodying this new way of
(45) seeing through distinctive treatment of light, color, and form.

Even if we grant that van Meegeren, with his undoubted mastery of Vermeer's innovative techniques, produced an aesthetically superior
(50) painting, he did so about three centuries after Vermeer developed the techniques in question. Whereas Vermeer's origination of these techniques in the seventeenth century represents a truly impressive and historic achievement, van Meegeren's production
(55) of *The Disciples at Emmaus* in the twentieth century presents nothing new or creative to the history of art. Van Meegeren's forgery therefore, for all its aesthetic merits, lacks the historical significance that makes Vermeer's work artistically great.

7. Which one of the following most accurately expresses the main point of the passage?

(A) *The Disciples at Emmaus*, van Meegeren's forgery of a Vermeer, was a failure in both aesthetic and artistic terms.

(B) The aesthetic value of a work of art is less dependent on the work's visible characteristics than on certain intangible characteristics.

(C) Forged artworks are artistically inferior to originals because artistic value depends in large part on originality of vision.

(D) The most skilled forgers can deceive even highly qualified art experts into accepting their work as original.

(E) Art critics tend to be unreliable judges of the aesthetic and artistic quality of works of art.

8. The passage provides the strongest support for inferring that Lessing holds which one of the following views?

(A) The judgments of critics who pronounced *The Disciples at Emmaus* to be aesthetically superb were not invalidated by the revelation that the painting is a forgery.

(B) The financial value of a work of art depends more on its purely aesthetic qualities than on its originality.

(C) Museum curators would be better off not taking art critics' opinions into account when attempting to determine whether a work of art is authentic.

(D) Because it is such a skilled imitation of Vermeer, *The Disciples at Emmaus* is as artistically successful as are original paintings by artists who are less significant than Vermeer.

(E) Works of art that have little or no aesthetic value can still be said to be great achievements in artistic terms.

9. In the first paragraph, the author refers to a highly reputed critic's persistence in believing van Meegeren's forgery to be a genuine Vermeer primarily in order to

(A) argue that many art critics are inflexible in their judgments

(B) indicate that the critics who initially praised *The Disciples at Emmaus* were not as knowledgeable as they appeared

(C) suggest that the painting may yet turn out to be a genuine Vermeer

(D) emphasize that the concept of forgery itself is internally incoherent

(E) illustrate the difficulties that skillfully executed forgeries can pose for art critics

GO ON TO THE NEXT PAGE.

10. The reaction described in which one of the following scenarios is most analogous to the reaction of the art critics mentioned in line 13?

(A) lovers of a musical group contemptuously reject a tribute album recorded by various other musicians as a second-rate imitation

(B) art historians extol the work of a little-known painter as innovative until it is discovered that the painter lived much more recently than was originally thought

(C) diners at a famous restaurant effusively praise the food as delicious until they learn that the master chef is away for the night

(D) literary critics enthusiastically applaud a new novel until its author reveals that its central symbols are intended to represent political views that the critics dislike

(E) movie fans evaluate a particular movie more favorably than they otherwise might have because their favorite actor plays the lead role

11. The passage provides the strongest support for inferring that Lessing holds which one of the following views?

(A) It is probable that many paintings currently hanging in important museums are actually forgeries.

(B) The historical circumstances surrounding the creation of a work are important in assessing the artistic value of that work.

(C) The greatness of an innovative artist depends on how much influence he or she has on other artists.

(D) The standards according to which a work is judged to be a forgery tend to vary from one historical period to another.

(E) An artist who makes use of techniques developed by others cannot be said to be innovative.

12. The passage most strongly supports which one of the following statements?

(A) In any historical period, the criteria by which a work is classified as a forgery can be a matter of considerable debate.

(B) An artist who uses techniques that others have developed is most likely a forger.

(C) A successful forger must originate a new artistic vision.

(D) Works of art created early in the career of a great artist are more likely than those created later to embody historic innovations.

(E) A painting can be a forgery even if it is not a copy of a particular original work of art.

13. Which one of the following, if true, would most strengthen Lessing's contention that a painting can display aesthetic excellence without possessing an equally high degree of artistic value?

(A) Many of the most accomplished art forgers have had moderately successful careers as painters of original works.

(B) Reproductions painted by talented young artists whose traditional training consisted in the copying of masterpieces were often seen as beautiful, but never regarded as great art.

(C) While experts can detect most forgeries, they can be duped by a talented forger who knows exactly what characteristics experts expect to find in the work of a particular painter.

(D) Most attempts at art forgery are ultimately unsuccessful because the forger has not mastered the necessary techniques.

(E) The criteria by which aesthetic excellence is judged change significantly from one century to another and from one culture to another.

GO ON TO THE NEXT PAGE.

Passage A

One function of language is to influence others' behavior by changing what they know, believe, or desire. For humans engaged in conversation, the perception of another's mental state is perhaps the
(5) most common vocalization stimulus.

While animal vocalizations may have evolved because they can potentially alter listeners' behavior to the signaler's benefit, such communication is—in contrast to human language—inadvertent, because
(10) most animals, with the possible exception of chimpanzees, cannot attribute mental states to others. The male *Physalaemus* frog calls because calling causes females to approach and other males to retreat, but there is no evidence that he does so because he attributes knowledge
(15) or desire to other frogs, or because he knows his calls will affect their knowledge and that this knowledge will, in turn, affect their behavior. Research also suggests that, in marked contrast to humans, nonhuman primates do not produce vocalizations in response to perception
(20) of another's need for information. Macaques, for example, give alarm calls when predators approach and coo calls upon finding food, yet experiments reveal no evidence that individuals were more likely to call about these events when they were aware of them but their offspring
(25) were clearly ignorant; similarly, chimpanzees do not appear to adjust their calling to inform ignorant individuals of their own location or that of food. Many animal vocalizations whose production initially seems goal-directed are not as purposeful as they first appear.

Passage B

(30) Many scientists distinguish animal communication systems from human language on the grounds that the former are rigid responses to stimuli, whereas human language is spontaneous and creative.

In this connection, it is commonly stated that no
(35) animal can use its communication system to lie. Obviously, a lie requires intention to deceive: to judge whether a particular instance of animal communication is truly prevarication requires knowledge of the animal's intentions. Language philosopher H. P. Grice explains
(40) that for an individual to mean something by uttering *x*, the individual must intend, in expressing *x*, to induce an audience to believe something and must also intend the utterance to be recognized as so intended. But conscious intention is a category of mental experience
(45) widely believed to be uniquely human. Philosopher Jacques Maritain's discussion of the honeybee's elaborate "waggle-dance" exemplifies this view. Although bees returning to the hive communicate to other bees the distance and direction of food sources,
(50) such communication is, Maritain asserts, merely a conditioned reflex: animals may use communicative signs but lack conscious intention regarding their use.

But these arguments are circular: conscious intention is ruled out a priori and then its absence
(55) taken as evidence that animal communication is fundamentally different from human language. In fact, the narrowing of the perceived gap between animal communication and human language revealed by recent research with chimpanzees and other animals
(60) calls into question not only the assumption that the difference between animal and human communication is qualitative rather than merely quantitative, but also the accompanying assumption that animals respond mechanically to stimuli, whereas humans speak with
(65) conscious understanding and intent.

14. Both passages are primarily concerned with addressing which one of the following questions?

(A) Are animals capable of deliberately prevaricating in order to achieve specific goals?

(B) Are the communications of animals characterized by conscious intention?

(C) What kinds of stimuli are most likely to elicit animal vocalizations?

(D) Are the communication systems of nonhuman primates qualitatively different from those of all other animals?

(E) Is there a scientific consensus about the differences between animal communication systems and human language?

15. In discussing the philosopher Maritain, the author of passage B seeks primarily to

(A) describe an interpretation of animal communication that the author believes rests on a logical error

(B) suggest by illustration that there is conscious intention underlying the communicative signs employed by certain animals

(C) present an argument in support of the view that animal communication systems are spontaneous and creative

(D) furnish specific evidence against the theory that most animal communication is merely a conditioned reflex

(E) point to a noted authority on animal communication whose views the author regards with respect

GO ON TO THE NEXT PAGE.

16. The author of passage B would be most likely to agree with which one of the following statements regarding researchers who subscribe to the position articulated in passage A?

    (A)   They fail to recognize that humans often communicate without any clear idea of their listeners' mental states.
    (B)   Most of them lack the credentials needed to assess the relevant experimental evidence correctly.
    (C)   They ignore well-known evidence that animals do in fact practice deception.
    (D)   They make assumptions about matters that should be determined empirically.
    (E)   They falsely believe that all communication systems can be explained in terms of their evolutionary benefits.

17. Which one of the following assertions from passage A provides support for the view attributed to Maritain in passage B (lines 50–52)?

    (A)   One function of language is to influence the behavior of others by changing what they think.
    (B)   Animal vocalizations may have evolved because they have the potential to alter listeners' behavior to the signaler's benefit.
    (C)   It is possible that chimpanzees may have the capacity to attribute mental states to others.
    (D)   There is no evidence that the male *Physalaemus* frog calls because he knows that his calls will affect the knowledge of other frogs.
    (E)   Macaques give alarm calls when predators approach and coo calls upon finding food.

18. The authors would be most likely to disagree over

    (A)   the extent to which communication among humans involves the ability to perceive the mental states of others
    (B)   the importance of determining to what extent animal communication systems differ from human language
    (C)   whether human language and animal communication differ from one another qualitatively or merely in a matter of degree
    (D)   whether chimpanzees' vocalizations suggest that they may possess the capacity to attribute mental states to others
    (E)   whether animals' vocalizations evolved to alter the behavior of other animals in a way that benefits the signaler

19. Passage B differs from passage A in that passage B is more

    (A)   optimistic regarding the ability of science to answer certain fundamental questions
    (B)   disapproving of the approach taken by others writing on the same general topic
    (C)   open-minded in its willingness to accept the validity of apparently conflicting positions
    (D)   supportive of ongoing research related to the question at hand
    (E)   circumspect in its refusal to commit itself to any positions with respect to still-unsettled research questions

GO ON TO THE NEXT PAGE.

In contrast to the mainstream of U.S. historiography during the late nineteenth and early twentieth centuries, African American historians of the period, such as George Washington Williams and
(5) W. E. B. DuBois, adopted a transnational perspective. This was true for several reasons, not the least of which was the necessity of doing so if certain aspects of the history of African Americans in the United States were to be treated honestly.
(10) First, there was the problem of citizenship. Even after the adoption in 1868 of the Fourteenth Amendment to the U.S. Constitution, which defined citizenship, the question of citizenship for African Americans had not been genuinely resolved. Because
(15) of this, emigrationist sentiment was a central issue in black political discourse, and both issues were critical topics for investigation. The implications for historical scholarship and national identity were enormous. While some black leaders insisted on their right to U.S.
(20) citizenship, others called on black people to emigrate and find a homeland of their own. Most African Americans were certainly not willing to relinquish their claims to the benefits of U.S. citizenship, but many had reached a point of profound pessimism and had
(25) begun to question their allegiance to the United States.
Mainstream U.S. historiography was firmly rooted in a nationalist approach during this period; the glorification of the nation and a focus on the nation-state as a historical force were dominant. The
(30) expanding spheres of influence of Europe and the United States prompted the creation of new genealogies of nations, new myths about the inevitability of nations, their "temperaments," their destinies. African American intellectuals who
(35) confronted the nationalist approach to historiography were troubled by its implications. Some argued that imperialism was a natural outgrowth of nationalism and its view that a state's strength is measured by the extension of its political power over colonial territory;
(40) the scramble for colonial empires was a distinct aspect of nationalism in the latter part of the nineteenth century.
Yet, for all their distrust of U.S. nationalism, most early black historians were themselves engaged in a
(45) sort of nation building. Deliberately or not, they contributed to the formation of a collective identity, reconstructing a glorious African past for the purposes of overturning degrading representations of blackness and establishing a firm cultural basis for a
(50) shared identity. Thus, one might argue that black historians' internationalism was a manifestation of a kind of nationalism that posits a diasporic community, which, while lacking a sovereign territory or official language, possesses a single culture, however
(55) mythical, with singular historical roots. Many members of this diaspora saw themselves as an oppressed "nation" without a homeland, or they imagined Africa as home. Hence, these historians understood their task to be the writing of the history
(60) of a people scattered by force and circumstance, a history that began in Africa.

20. Which one of the following most accurately expresses the main idea of the passage?

(A) Historians are now recognizing that the major challenge faced by African Americans in the late nineteenth and early twentieth centuries was the struggle for citizenship.

(B) Early African American historians who practiced a transnational approach to history were primarily interested in advancing an emigrationist project.

(C) U.S. historiography in the late nineteenth and early twentieth centuries was characterized by a conflict between African American historians who viewed history from a transnational perspective and mainstream historians who took a nationalist perspective.

(D) The transnational perspective of early African American historians countered mainstream nationalist historiography, but it was arguably nationalist itself to the extent that it posited a culturally unified diasporic community.

(E) Mainstream U.S. historians in the late nineteenth and early twentieth centuries could no longer justify their nationalist approach to history once they were confronted with the transnational perspective taken by African American historians.

21. Which one of the following phrases most accurately conveys the sense of the word "reconstructing" as it is used in line 47?

(A) correcting a misconception about
(B) determining the sequence of events in
(C) investigating the implications of
(D) rewarding the promoters of
(E) shaping a conception of

22. Which one of the following is most strongly supported by the passage?

(A) Emigrationist sentiment would not have been as strong among African Americans in the late nineteenth century had the promise of U.S. citizenship been fully realized for African Americans at that time.

(B) Scholars writing the history of diasporic communities generally do not discuss the forces that initially caused the scattering of the members of those communities.

(C) Most historians of the late nineteenth and early twentieth centuries endeavored to make the histories of the nations about which they wrote seem more glorious than they actually were.

(D) To be properly considered nationalist, a historical work must ignore the ways in which one nation's foreign policy decisions affected other nations.

(E) A considerable number of early African American historians embraced nationalism and the inevitability of the dominance of the nation-state.

GO ON TO THE NEXT PAGE.

23. As it is described in the passage, the transnational approach employed by African American historians working in the late nineteenth and early twentieth centuries would be best exemplified by a historical study that

(A) investigated the extent to which European and U.S. nationalist mythologies contradicted one another

(B) defined the national characters of the United States and several European nations by focusing on their treatment of minority populations rather than on their territorial ambitions

(C) recounted the attempts by the United States to gain control over new territories during the late nineteenth and early twentieth centuries

(D) considered the impact of emigrationist sentiment among African Americans on U.S. foreign policy in Africa during the late nineteenth century

(E) examined the extent to which African American culture at the turn of the century incorporated traditions that were common to a number of African cultures

24. The passage provides information sufficient to answer which one of the following questions?

(A) Which African nations did early African American historians research in writing their histories of the African diaspora?

(B) What were some of the African languages spoken by the ancestors of the members of the African diasporic community who were living in the United States in the late nineteenth century?

(C) Over which territories abroad did the United States attempt to extend its political power in the latter part of the nineteenth century?

(D) Are there textual ambiguities in the Fourteenth Amendment that spurred the conflict over U.S. citizenship for African Americans?

(E) In what ways did African American leaders respond to the question of citizenship for African Americans in the latter part of the nineteenth century?

25. The author of the passage would be most likely to agree with which one of the following statements?

(A) Members of a particular diasporic community have a common country of origin.

(B) Territorial sovereignty is not a prerequisite for the project of nation building.

(C) Early African American historians who rejected nationalist historiography declined to engage in historical myth-making of any kind.

(D) The most prominent African American historians in the late nineteenth and early twentieth centuries advocated emigration for African Americans.

(E) Historians who employed a nationalist approach focused on entirely different events from those studied and written about by early African American historians.

26. The main purpose of the second paragraph of the passage is to

(A) explain why early African American historians felt compelled to approach historiography in the way that they did

(B) show that governmental actions such as constitutional amendments do not always have the desired effect

(C) support the contention that African American intellectuals in the late nineteenth century were critical of U.S. imperialism

(D) establish that some African American political leaders in the late nineteenth century advocated emigration as an alternative to fighting for the benefits of U.S. citizenship

(E) argue that the definition of citizenship contained in the Fourteenth Amendment to the U.S. Constitution is too limited

27. As it is presented in the passage, the approach to history taken by mainstream U.S. historians of the late nineteenth and early twentieth centuries is most similar to the approach exemplified in which one of the following?

(A) An elected official writes a memo suggesting that because a particular course of action has been successful in the past, the government should continue to pursue that course of action.

(B) A biographer of a famous novelist argues that the precocity apparent in certain of the novelist's early achievements confirms that her success was attributable to innate talent.

(C) A doctor maintains that because a certain medication was developed expressly for the treatment of an illness, it is the best treatment for that illness.

(D) A newspaper runs a series of articles in order to inform the public about the environmentally hazardous practices of a large corporation.

(E) A scientist gets the same result from an experiment several times and therefore concludes that its chemical reactions always proceed in the observed fashion.

S T O P
IF YOU FINISH BEFORE TIME IS CALLED, YOU MAY CHECK YOUR WORK ON THIS SECTION ONLY.
DO NOT WORK ON ANY OTHER SECTION IN THE TEST.

SECTION II

Time—35 minutes

25 Questions

Directions: The questions in this section are based on the reasoning contained in brief statements or passages. For some questions, more than one of the choices could conceivably answer the question. However, you are to choose the best answer; that is, the response that most accurately and completely answers the question. You should not make assumptions that are by commonsense standards implausible, superfluous, or incompatible with the passage. After you have chosen the best answer, blacken the corresponding space on your answer sheet.

1. Mary to Jamal: You acknowledge that as the legitimate owner of this business I have the legal right to sell it whenever I wish. But also you claim that because loyal employees will suffer if I sell it, I therefore have no right to do so. Obviously, your statements taken together are absurd.

Mary's reasoning is most vulnerable to the criticism that she

(A) overlooks the possibility that when Jamal claims that she has no right to sell the business, he simply means she has no right to do so at this time

(B) overlooks the possibility that her employees also have rights related to the sale of the business

(C) provides no evidence for the claim that she does have a right to sell the business

(D) overlooks the possibility that Jamal is referring to two different kinds of right

(E) attacks Jamal's character rather than his argument

2. Since there is no survival value in an animal's having an organ that is able to function when all its other organs have broken down to such a degree that the animal dies, it is a result of the efficiency of natural selection that no organ is likely to evolve in such a way that it greatly outlasts the body's other organs.

Of the following, which one illustrates a principle that is most similar to the principle illustrated by the passage?

(A) A store in a lower-income neighborhood finds that it is unable to sell its higher-priced goods and so stocks them only when ordered by a customer.

(B) The body of an animal with a deficient organ is often able to compensate for that deficiency when other organs perform the task the deficient one normally performs.

(C) One car model produced by an automobile manufacturer has a life expectancy that is so much longer than its other models that its great popularity requires the manufacturer to stop producing some of the other models.

(D) Athletes occasionally overdevelop some parts of their bodies to such a great extent that other parts of their bodies are more prone to injury as a result.

(E) Automotive engineers find that it is not cost-effective to manufacture a given automobile part of such high quality that it outlasts all other parts of the automobile, as doing so would not raise the overall quality of the automobile.

GO ON TO THE NEXT PAGE.

3. Commentator: If a political administration is both economically successful and successful at protecting individual liberties, then it is an overall success. Even an administration that fails to care for the environment may succeed overall if it protects individual liberties. So far, the present administration has not cared for the environment but has successfully protected individual liberties.

    If all of the statements above are true, then which one of the following must be true?

    (A) The present administration is economically successful.
    (B) The present administration is not an overall success.
    (C) If the present administration is economically successful, then it is an overall success.
    (D) If the present administration had been economically successful, it would have cared for the environment.
    (E) If the present administration succeeds at environmental protection, then it will be an overall success.

4. The legislature is considering a proposed bill that would prohibit fishing in Eagle Bay. Despite widespread concern over the economic effect this ban would have on the local fishing industry, the bill should be enacted. The bay has one of the highest water pollution levels in the nation, and a recent study of the bay's fish found that 80 percent of them contained toxin levels that exceed governmental safety standards. Continuing to permit fishing in Eagle Bay could thus have grave effects on public health.

    The argument proceeds by presenting evidence that

    (A) the toxic contamination of fish in Eagle Bay has had grave economic effects on the local fishing industry
    (B) the moral principle that an action must be judged on the basis of its foreseeable effects is usually correct
    (C) the opponents of the ban have failed to weigh properly its foreseeable negative effects against its positive ones
    (D) failure to enact the ban would carry with it unacceptable risks for the public welfare
    (E) the ban would reduce the level of toxins in the fish in Eagle Bay

5. Vandenburg: This art museum is not adhering to its purpose. Its founders intended it to devote as much attention to contemporary art as to the art of earlier periods, but its collection of contemporary art is far smaller than its other collections.

    Simpson: The relatively small size of the museum's contemporary art collection is appropriate. It's an art museum, not an ethnographic museum designed to collect every style of every period. Its contemporary art collection is small because its curators believe that there is little high-quality contemporary art.

    Which one of the following principles, if valid, most helps to justify the reasoning in Simpson's response to Vandenburg?

    (A) An art museum should collect only works that its curators consider to be of high artistic quality.
    (B) An art museum should not collect any works that violate the purpose defined by the museum's founders.
    (C) An art museum's purpose need not be to collect every style of every period.
    (D) An ethnographic museum's purpose should be defined according to its curators' beliefs.
    (E) The intentions of an art museum's curators should not determine what is collected by that museum.

6. Over the last five years, every new major alternative-energy initiative that initially was promised government funding has since seen that funding severely curtailed. In no such case has the government come even close to providing the level of funds initially earmarked for these projects. Since large corporations have made it a point to discourage alternative-energy projects, it is likely that the corporations' actions influenced the government's funding decisions.

    Which one of the following, if true, most strengthens the reasoning above?

    (A) For the past two decades, most alternative-energy initiatives have received little or no government funding.
    (B) The funding initially earmarked for a government project is always subject to change, given the mechanisms by which the political process operates.
    (C) The only research projects whose government funding has been severely curtailed are those that large corporations have made it a point to discourage.
    (D) Some projects encouraged by large corporations have seen their funding severely curtailed over the last five years.
    (E) All large corporations have made it a point to discourage some forms of research.

GO ON TO THE NEXT PAGE.

7. Talbert: Chess is beneficial for school-age children. It
    is enjoyable, encourages foresight and logical
    thinking, and discourages carelessness, inattention,
    and impulsiveness. In short, it promotes mental
    maturity.

    Sklar: My objection to teaching chess to children is that
    it diverts mental activity from something with
    societal value, such as science, into something that
    has no societal value.

    Talbert's and Sklar's statements provide the strongest
    support for holding that they disagree with each other
    over whether

    (A)   chess promotes mental maturity
    (B)   many activities promote mental maturity just as
          well as chess does
    (C)   chess is socially valuable and science is not
    (D)   children should be taught to play chess
    (E)   children who neither play chess nor study science
          are mentally immature

8. Marcia: Not all vegetarian diets lead to nutritional
    deficiencies. Research shows that vegetarians can
    obtain a full complement of proteins and minerals
    from nonanimal foods.

    Theodora: You are wrong in claiming that vegetarianism
    cannot lead to nutritional deficiencies. If most
    people became vegetarians, some of those losing
    jobs due to the collapse of many meat-based
    industries would fall into poverty and hence be
    unable to afford a nutritionally adequate diet.

    Theodora's reply to Marcia's argument is most vulnerable
    to criticism on the grounds that her reply

    (A)   is directed toward disproving a claim that Marcia
          did not make
    (B)   ignores the results of the research cited by Marcia
    (C)   takes for granted that no meat-based industries
          will collapse unless most people become
          vegetarians
    (D)   uses the word "diet" in a nontechnical sense
          whereas Marcia's argument uses this term in a
          medical sense
    (E)   takes for granted that people losing jobs in meat-
          based industries would become vegetarians

9. Musicologist: Classification of a musical instrument
    depends on the mechanical action through which
    it produces music. So the piano is properly called
    a percussion instrument, not a stringed instrument.
    Even though the vibration of the piano's strings
    is what makes its sound, the strings are caused to
    vibrate by the impact of hammers.

    Which one of the following most accurately expresses the
    main conclusion of the musicologist's argument?

    (A)   Musical instruments should be classified
          according to the mechanical actions through
          which they produce sound.
    (B)   Musical instruments should not be classified
          based on the way musicians interact with them.
    (C)   Some people classify the piano as a stringed
          instrument because of the way the piano
          produces sound.
    (D)   The piano should be classified as a stringed
          instrument rather than as a percussion
          instrument.
    (E)   It is correct to classify the piano as a percussion
          instrument rather than as a stringed instrument.

10. In a vast ocean region, phosphorus levels have doubled
    in the past few decades due to agricultural runoff pouring
    out of a large river nearby. The phosphorus stimulates
    the growth of plankton near the ocean surface. Decaying
    plankton fall to the ocean floor, where bacteria devour
    them, consuming oxygen in the process. Due to the
    resulting oxygen depletion, few fish can survive in this
    region.

    Which one of the following can be properly inferred from
    the information above?

    (A)   The agricultural runoff pouring out of the river
          contributes to the growth of plankton near the
          ocean surface.
    (B)   Before phosphorus levels doubled in the ocean
          region, most fish were able to survive in that
          region.
    (C)   If agricultural runoff ceased pouring out of the
          river, there would be no bacteria on the ocean
          floor devouring decaying plankton.
    (D)   The quantity of agricultural runoff pouring out of
          the river has doubled in the past few decades.
    (E)   The amount of oxygen in a body of water is in
          general inversely proportional to the level of
          phosphorus in that body of water.

GO ON TO THE NEXT PAGE.

11. Psychologists observing a shopping mall parking lot found that, on average, drivers spent 39 seconds leaving a parking space when another car was quietly waiting to enter it, 51 seconds if the driver of the waiting car honked impatiently, but only 32 seconds leaving a space when no one was waiting. This suggests that drivers feel possessive of their parking spaces even when leaving them, and that this possessiveness increases in reaction to indications that another driver wants the space.

Which one of the following, if true, most weakens the reasoning?

(A) The more pressure most drivers feel because others are waiting for them to perform maneuvers with their cars, the less quickly they are able to perform them.

(B) The amount of time drivers spend entering a parking space is not noticeably affected by whether other drivers are waiting for them to do so, nor by whether those other drivers are honking impatiently.

(C) It is considerably more difficult and time-consuming for a driver to maneuver a car out of a parking space if another car waiting to enter that space is nearby.

(D) Parking spaces in shopping mall parking lots are unrepresentative of parking spaces in general with respect to the likelihood that other cars will be waiting to enter them.

(E) Almost any driver leaving a parking space will feel angry at another driver who honks impatiently, and this anger will influence the amount of time spent leaving the space.

12. Shark teeth are among the most common vertebrate fossils; yet fossilized shark skeletons are much less common—indeed, comparatively rare among fossilized vertebrate skeletons.

Which one of the following, if true, most helps to resolve the apparent paradox described above?

(A) Unlike the bony skeletons of other vertebrates, shark skeletons are composed of cartilage, and teeth and bone are much more likely to fossilize than cartilage is.

(B) The rare fossilized skeletons of sharks that are found are often found in areas other than those in which fossils of shark teeth are plentiful.

(C) Fossils of sharks' teeth are quite difficult to distinguish from fossils of other kinds of teeth.

(D) Some species of sharks alive today grow and lose many sets of teeth during their lifetimes.

(E) The physical and chemical processes involved in the fossilization of sharks' teeth are as common as those involved in the fossilization of shark skeletons.

13. Critic: Photographers, by deciding which subjects to depict and how to depict them, express their own worldviews in their photographs, however realistically those photographs may represent reality. Thus, photographs are interpretations of reality.

The argument's conclusion is properly drawn if which one of the following is assumed?

(A) Even representing a subject realistically can involve interpreting that subject.

(B) To express a worldview is to interpret reality.

(C) All visual art expresses the artist's worldview.

(D) Any interpretation of reality involves the expression of a worldview.

(E) Nonrealistic photographs, like realistic photographs, express the worldviews of the photographers who take them.

14. Geologists recently discovered marks that closely resemble worm tracks in a piece of sandstone. These marks were made more than half a billion years earlier than the earliest known traces of multicellular animal life. Therefore, the marks are probably the traces of geological processes rather than of worms.

Which one of the following, if true, most weakens the argument?

(A) It is sometimes difficult to estimate the precise age of a piece of sandstone.

(B) Geological processes left a substantial variety of marks in sandstone more than half a billion years before the earliest known multicellular animal life existed.

(C) There were some early life forms other than worms that are known to have left marks that are hard to distinguish from those found in the piece of sandstone.

(D) At the place where the sandstone was found, the only geological processes that are likely to mark sandstone in ways that resemble worm tracks could not have occurred at the time the marks were made.

(E) Most scientists knowledgeable about early animal life believe that worms are likely to have been among the earliest forms of multicellular animal life on Earth, but evidence of their earliest existence is scarce because they are composed solely of soft tissue.

GO ON TO THE NEXT PAGE.

15. Often a type of organ or body structure is the only physically feasible means of accomplishing a given task, so it should be unsurprising if, like eyes or wings, that type of organ or body structure evolves at different times in a number of completely unrelated species. After all, whatever the difference of heritage and habitat, as organisms animals have fundamentally similar needs and so _____.

Which one of the following most logically completes the last sentence of the passage?

(A) will often live in the same environment as other species quite different from themselves

(B) will in many instances evolve similar adaptations enabling them to satisfy these needs

(C) will develop adaptations allowing them to satisfy these needs

(D) will resemble other species having different biological needs

(E) will all develop eyes or wings as adaptations

16. Engineer: Thermophotovoltaic generators are devices that convert heat into electricity. The process of manufacturing steel produces huge amounts of heat that currently go to waste. So if steel-manufacturing plants could feed the heat they produce into thermophotovoltaic generators, they would greatly reduce their electric bills, thereby saving money.

Which one of the following is an assumption on which the engineer's argument depends?

(A) There is no other means of utilizing the heat produced by the steel-manufacturing process that would be more cost effective than installing thermophotovoltaic generators.

(B) Using current technology, it would be possible for steel-manufacturing plants to feed the heat they produce into thermophotovoltaic generators in such a way that those generators could convert at least some of that heat into electricity.

(C) The amount steel-manufacturing plants would save on their electric bills by feeding heat into thermophotovoltaic generators would be sufficient to cover the cost of purchasing and installing those generators.

(D) At least some steel-manufacturing plants rely on electricity as their primary source of energy in the steel-manufacturing process.

(E) There are at least some steel-manufacturing plants that could greatly reduce their electricity bills only if they used some method of converting wasted heat or other energy from the steel-manufacturing process into electricity.

17. Herbalist: While standard antibiotics typically have just one active ingredient, herbal antibacterial remedies typically contain several. Thus, such herbal remedies are more likely to retain their effectiveness against new, resistant strains of bacteria than are standard antibiotics. For a strain of bacteria, the difficulty of developing resistance to an herbal antibacterial remedy is like a cook's difficulty in trying to prepare a single meal that will please all of several dozen guests, a task far more difficult than preparing one meal that will please a single guest.

In the analogy drawn in the argument above, which one of the following corresponds to a standard antibiotic?

(A) a single guest
(B) several dozen guests
(C) the pleasure experienced by a single guest
(D) a cook
(E) the ingredients available to a cook

18. To find out how barn owls learn how to determine the direction from which sounds originate, scientists put distorting lenses over the eyes of young barn owls before the owls first opened their eyes. The owls with these lenses behaved as if objects making sounds were farther to the right than they actually were. Once the owls matured, the lenses were removed, yet the owls continued to act as if they misjudged the location of the source of sounds. The scientists consequently hypothesized that once a barn owl has developed an auditory scheme for estimating the point from which sounds originate, it ceases to use vision to locate sounds.

The scientists' reasoning is vulnerable to which one of the following criticisms?

(A) It fails to consider whether the owls' vision was permanently impaired by their having worn the lenses while immature.

(B) It assumes that the sense of sight is equally good in all owls.

(C) It attributes human reasoning processes to a nonhuman organism.

(D) It neglects to consider how similar distorting lenses might affect the behavior of other bird species.

(E) It uses as evidence experimental results that were irrelevant to the conclusion.

GO ON TO THE NEXT PAGE.

19. As often now as in the past, newspaper journalists use direct or indirect quotation to report unsupported or false claims made by newsmakers. However, journalists are becoming less likely to openly challenge the veracity of such claims within their articles.

Each of the following, if true, helps to explain the trend in journalism described above EXCEPT:

(A) Newspaper publishers have found that many readers will cancel a subscription simply because a view they take for granted has been disputed by the publication.

(B) The areas of knowledge on which journalists report are growing in specialization and diversity, while journalists themselves are not becoming more broadly knowledgeable.

(C) Persons supporting controversial views more and more frequently choose to speak only to reporters who seem sympathetic to their views.

(D) A basic principle of journalism holds that debate over controversial issues draws the attention of the public.

(E) Journalists who challenge the veracity of claims are often criticized for failing their professional obligation to be objective.

20. When people show signs of having a heart attack an electrocardiograph (EKG) is often used to diagnose their condition. In a study, a computer program for EKG diagnosis of heart attacks was pitted against a very experienced, highly skilled cardiologist. The program correctly diagnosed a significantly higher proportion of the cases that were later confirmed to be heart attacks than did the cardiologist. Interpreting EKG data, therefore, should be left to computer programs.

Which one of the following, if true, most weakens the argument?

(A) Experts agreed that the cardiologist made few obvious mistakes in reading and interpreting the EKG data.

(B) The practice of medicine is as much an art as a science, and computer programs are not easily adapted to making subjective judgments.

(C) The cardiologist correctly diagnosed a significantly higher proportion of the cases in which no heart attack occurred than did the computer program.

(D) In a considerable percentage of cases, EKG data alone are insufficient to enable either computer programs or cardiologists to make accurate diagnoses.

(E) The cardiologist in the study was unrepresentative of cardiologists in general with respect to skill and experience.

21. A government study indicates that raising speed limits to reflect the actual average speeds of traffic on level, straight stretches of high-speed roadways reduces the accident rate. Since the actual average speed for level, straight stretches of high-speed roadways tends to be 120 kilometers per hour (75 miles per hour), that should be set as a uniform national speed limit for level, straight stretches of all such roadways.

Which one of the following principles, if valid, most helps to justify the reasoning above?

(A) Uniform national speed limits should apply only to high-speed roadways.

(B) Traffic laws applying to high-speed roadways should apply uniformly across the nation.

(C) A uniform national speed limit for high-speed roadways should be set only if all such roadways have roughly equal average speeds of traffic.

(D) Long-standing laws that are widely violated are probably not good laws.

(E) Any measure that reduces the rate of traffic accidents should be implemented.

GO ON TO THE NEXT PAGE.

22. Psychiatrist: In treating first-year students at this university, I have noticed that those reporting the highest levels of spending on recreation score at about the same level on standard screening instruments for anxiety and depression as those reporting the lowest levels of spending on recreation. This suggests that the first-year students with high levels of spending on recreation could reduce that spending without increasing their anxiety or depression.

Each of the following, if true, strengthens the psychiatrist's argument EXCEPT:

(A)   At other universities, first-year students reporting the highest levels of spending on recreation also show the same degree of anxiety and depression as do those reporting the lowest levels of such spending.

(B)   Screening of first-year students at the university who report moderate levels of spending on recreation reveals that those students are less anxious and depressed than both those with the highest and those with the lowest levels of spending on recreation.

(C)   Among adults between the ages of 40 and 60, increased levels of spending on recreation are strongly correlated with decreased levels of anxiety and depression.

(D)   The screening instruments used by the psychiatrist are extremely accurate in revealing levels of anxiety and depression among university students.

(E)   Several of the psychiatrist's patients who are first-year students at the university have reduced their spending on recreation from very high levels to very low levels without increasing their anxiety or depression.

23. Every brick house on River Street has a front yard. Most of the houses on River Street that have front yards also have two stories. So most of the brick houses on River Street have two stories.

Which one of the following is most appropriate as an analogy demonstrating that the reasoning in the argument above is flawed?

(A)   By that line of reasoning, we could conclude that most politicians have run for office, since all legislators are politicians and most legislators have run for office.

(B)   By that line of reasoning, we could conclude that most public servants are legislators, since most legislators have run for office and most politicians who have run for office are public servants.

(C)   By that line of reasoning, we could conclude that not every public servant has run for office, since every legislator is a public servant but some public servants are not legislators.

(D)   By that line of reasoning, we could conclude that most legislators have never run for office, since most public servants have never run for office and all legislators are public servants.

(E)   By that line of reasoning, we could conclude that most legislators are not public servants, since most public servants have not run for office and most legislators have run for office.

GO ON TO THE NEXT PAGE.

24. Historian: It is unlikely that someone would see history as the working out of moral themes unless he or she held clear and unambiguous moral beliefs. However, one's inclination to morally judge human behavior decreases as one's knowledge of history increases. Consequently, the more history a person knows, the less likely that person is to view history as the working out of moral themes.

The conclusion of the argument is properly drawn if which one of the following is assumed?

(A) Historical events that fail to elicit moral disapproval are generally not considered to exemplify a moral theme.

(B) The less inclined one is to morally judge human behavior, the less likely it is that one holds clear and unambiguous moral beliefs.

(C) Only those who do not understand human history attribute moral significance to historical events.

(D) The more clear and unambiguous one's moral beliefs, the more likely one is to view history as the working out of moral themes.

(E) People tend to be less objective regarding a subject about which they possess extensive knowledge than regarding a subject about which they do not possess extensive knowledge.

25. A recent poll revealed that most students at our university prefer that the university, which is searching for a new president, hire someone who has extensive experience as a university president. However, in the very same poll, the person most students chose from among a list of leading candidates as the one they would most like to see hired was someone who has never served as a university president.

Which one of the following, if true, most helps to account for the apparent discrepancy in the students' preferences?

(A) Because several of the candidates listed in the poll had extensive experience as university presidents, not all of the candidates could be differentiated on this basis alone.

(B) Most of the candidates listed in the poll had extensive experience as university presidents.

(C) Students taking the poll had fewer candidates to choose from than were currently being considered for the position.

(D) Most of the students taking the poll did not know whether any of the leading candidates listed in the poll had ever served as a university president.

(E) Often a person can be well suited to a position even though they have relatively little experience in such a position.

S T O P
IF YOU FINISH BEFORE TIME IS CALLED, YOU MAY CHECK YOUR WORK ON THIS SECTION ONLY.
DO NOT WORK ON ANY OTHER SECTION IN THE TEST.

SECTION III
Time—35 minutes
23 Questions

Directions: Each group of questions in this section is based on a set of conditions. In answering some of the questions, it may be useful to draw a rough diagram. Choose the response that most accurately and completely answers each question and blacken the corresponding space on your answer sheet.

Questions 1–5

Exactly six workers—Faith, Gus, Hannah, Juan, Kenneth, and Lisa—will travel to a business convention in two cars—car 1 and car 2. Each car must carry at least two of the workers, one of whom will be assigned to drive. For the entire trip, the workers will comply with an assignment that also meets the following constraints:

Either Faith or Gus must drive the car in which Hannah travels.
Either Faith or Kenneth must drive the car in which Juan travels.
Gus must travel in the same car as Lisa.

1. Which one of the following is a possible assignment of the workers to the cars?

    (A)   car 1: Faith (driver), Hannah, and Juan
           car 2: Gus (driver), Kenneth, and Lisa
    (B)   car 1: Faith (driver), Hannah, and Kenneth
           car 2: Lisa (driver), Gus, and Juan
    (C)   car 1: Faith (driver), Juan, Kenneth, and Lisa
           car 2: Gus (driver) and Hannah
    (D)   car 1: Faith (driver) and Juan
           car 2: Kenneth (driver), Gus, Hannah, and Lisa
    (E)   car 1: Gus (driver), Hannah, and Lisa
           car 2: Juan (driver), Faith, and Kenneth

2. The two workers who drive the cars CANNOT be

    (A)   Faith and Gus
    (B)   Faith and Kenneth
    (C)   Faith and Lisa
    (D)   Gus and Kenneth
    (E)   Kenneth and Lisa

3. If Lisa drives one of the cars, then which one of the following could be true?

    (A)   Faith travels in the same car as Kenneth.
    (B)   Faith travels in the same car as Lisa.
    (C)   Gus travels in the same car as Hannah.
    (D)   Gus travels in the same car as Juan.
    (E)   Hannah travels in the same car as Lisa.

4. If Faith travels with two other workers in car 1, and if Faith is not the driver, then the person in car 1 other than Faith and the driver must be

    (A)   Gus
    (B)   Hannah
    (C)   Juan
    (D)   Kenneth
    (E)   Lisa

5. Which one of the following CANNOT be true?

    (A)   Gus is the only person other than the driver in one of the cars.
    (B)   Hannah is the only person other than the driver in one of the cars.
    (C)   Juan is the only person other than the driver in one of the cars.
    (D)   Kenneth is the only person other than the driver in one of the cars.
    (E)   Lisa is the only person other than the driver in one of the cars.

GO ON TO THE NEXT PAGE.

Questions 6–11

An archaeologist has six ancient artifacts—a figurine, a headdress, a jar, a necklace, a plaque, and a tureen—no two of which are the same age. She will order them from first (oldest) to sixth (most recent). The following has already been determined:

The figurine is older than both the jar and the headdress.
The necklace and the jar are both older than the tureen.
Either the plaque is older than both the headdress and the necklace, or both the headdress and the necklace are older than the plaque.

6. Which one of the following could be the artifacts in the order of their age, from first to sixth?

(A)   figurine, headdress, jar, necklace, plaque, tureen
(B)   figurine, jar, plaque, headdress, tureen, necklace
(C)   figurine, necklace, plaque, headdress, jar, tureen
(D)   necklace, jar, figurine, headdress, plaque, tureen
(E)   plaque, tureen, figurine, necklace, jar, headdress

7. Exactly how many of the artifacts are there any one of which could be first?

(A)   one
(B)   two
(C)   three
(D)   four
(E)   five

8. Which one of the following artifacts CANNOT be fourth?

(A)   figurine
(B)   headdress
(C)   jar
(D)   necklace
(E)   plaque

9. If the figurine is third, which one of the following must be second?

(A)   headdress
(B)   jar
(C)   necklace
(D)   plaque
(E)   tureen

10. If the plaque is first, then exactly how many artifacts are there any one of which could be second?

(A)   one
(B)   two
(C)   three
(D)   four
(E)   five

11. Which one of the following, if substituted for the information that the necklace and the jar are both older than the tureen, would have the same effect in determining the order of the artifacts?

(A)   The tureen is older than the headdress but not as old as the figurine.
(B)   The figurine and the necklace are both older than the tureen.
(C)   The necklace is older than the tureen if and only if the jar is.
(D)   All of the artifacts except the headdress and the plaque must be older than the tureen.
(E)   The plaque is older than the necklace if and only if the plaque is older than the tureen.

GO ON TO THE NEXT PAGE.

Questions 12–17

The coach of a women's track team must determine which four of five runners—Quinn, Ramirez, Smith, Terrell, and Uzoma—will run in the four races of an upcoming track meet. Each of the four runners chosen will run in exactly one of the four races—the first, second, third, or fourth. The coach's selection is bound by the following constraints:

If Quinn runs in the track meet, then Terrell runs in the race immediately after the race in which Quinn runs.

Smith does not run in either the second race or the fourth race.

If Uzoma does not run in the track meet, then Ramirez runs in the second race.

If Ramirez runs in the second race, then Uzoma does not run in the track meet.

12. Which one of the following could be the order in which the runners run, from first to fourth?

(A) Uzoma, Ramirez, Quinn, Terrell
(B) Terrell, Smith, Ramirez, Uzoma
(C) Smith, Ramirez, Terrell, Quinn
(D) Ramirez, Uzoma, Smith, Terrell
(E) Quinn, Terrell, Smith, Ramirez

13. Which one of the following runners must the coach select to run in the track meet?

(A) Quinn
(B) Ramirez
(C) Smith
(D) Terrell
(E) Uzoma

14. The question of which runners will be chosen to run in the track meet and in what races they will run can be completely resolved if which one of the following is true?

(A) Ramirez runs in the first race.
(B) Ramirez runs in the second race.
(C) Ramirez runs in the third race.
(D) Ramirez runs in the fourth race.
(E) Ramirez does not run in the track meet.

15. Which one of the following CANNOT be true?

(A) Ramirez runs in the race immediately before the race in which Smith runs.
(B) Smith runs in the race immediately before the race in which Quinn runs.
(C) Smith runs in the race immediately before the race in which Terrell runs.
(D) Terrell runs in the race immediately before the race in which Ramirez runs.
(E) Uzoma runs in the race immediately before the race in which Terrell runs.

16. If Uzoma runs in the first race, then which one of the following must be true?

(A) Quinn does not run in the track meet.
(B) Smith does not run in the track meet.
(C) Quinn runs in the second race.
(D) Terrell runs in the second race.
(E) Ramirez runs in the fourth race.

17. If both Quinn and Smith run in the track meet, then how many of the runners are there any one of whom could be the one who runs in the first race?

(A) one
(B) two
(C) three
(D) four
(E) five

GO ON TO THE NEXT PAGE.

Questions 18–23

From the 1st through the 7th of next month, seven nurses—
Farnham, Griseldi, Heany, Juarez, Khan, Lightfoot, and
Moreau—will each conduct one information session at a
community center. Each nurse's session will fall on a different
day. The nurses' schedule is governed by the following
constraints:

  At least two of the other nurses' sessions must fall in
  between Heany's session and Moreau's session.
  Griseldi's session must be on the day before Khan's.
  Juarez's session must be on a later day than Moreau's.
  Farnham's session must be on an earlier day than Khan's
  but on a later day than Lightfoot's.
  Lightfoot cannot conduct the session on the 2nd.

18. Which one of the following could be the order of the
     nurses' sessions, from first to last?

     (A)   Farnham, Griseldi, Khan, Moreau, Juarez,
            Lightfoot, Heany
     (B)   Heany, Lightfoot, Farnham, Moreau, Juarez,
            Griseldi, Khan
     (C)   Juarez, Heany, Lightfoot, Farnham, Moreau,
            Griseldi, Khan
     (D)   Lightfoot, Moreau, Farnham, Juarez, Griseldi,
            Khan, Heany
     (E)   Moreau, Lightfoot, Heany, Juarez, Farnham,
            Griseldi, Khan

19. Juarez's session CANNOT be on which one of the
     following days?

     (A)   the 2nd
     (B)   the 3rd
     (C)   the 5th
     (D)   the 6th
     (E)   the 7th

20. If Juarez's session is on the 3rd, then which one of the
     following could be true?

     (A)   Moreau's session is on the 1st.
     (B)   Khan's session is on the 5th.
     (C)   Heany's session is on the 6th.
     (D)   Griseldi's session is on the 5th.
     (E)   Farnham's session is on the 2nd.

21. If Khan's session is on an earlier day than Moreau's,
     which one of the following could conduct the session on
     the 3rd?

     (A)   Griseldi
     (B)   Heany
     (C)   Juarez
     (D)   Lightfoot
     (E)   Moreau

22. If Griseldi's session is on the 5th, then which one of the
     following must be true?

     (A)   Farnham's session is on the 3rd.
     (B)   Heany's session is on the 7th.
     (C)   Juarez's session is on the 4th.
     (D)   Lightfoot's session is on the 1st.
     (E)   Moreau's session is on the 2nd.

23. Lightfoot's session could be on which one of the
     following days?

     (A)   the 3rd
     (B)   the 4th
     (C)   the 5th
     (D)   the 6th
     (E)   the 7th

S T O P
IF YOU FINISH BEFORE TIME IS CALLED, YOU MAY CHECK YOUR WORK ON THIS SECTION ONLY.
DO NOT WORK ON ANY OTHER SECTION IN THE TEST.

SECTION IV
Time—35 minutes
26 Questions

Directions: The questions in this section are based on the reasoning contained in brief statements or passages. For some questions, more than one of the choices could conceivably answer the question. However, you are to choose the best answer; that is, the response that most accurately and completely answers the question. You should not make assumptions that are by commonsense standards implausible, superfluous, or incompatible with the passage. After you have chosen the best answer, blacken the corresponding space on your answer sheet.

1. Among Trinidadian guppies, males with large spots are more attractive to females than are males with small spots, who consequently are presented with less frequent mating opportunities. Yet guppies with small spots are more likely to avoid detection by predators, so in waters where predators are abundant only guppies with small spots live to maturity.

The situation described above most closely conforms to which one of the following generalizations?

(A) A trait that helps attract mates is sometimes more dangerous to one sex than to another.
(B) Those organisms that are most attractive to the opposite sex have the greatest number of offspring.
(C) Those organisms that survive the longest have the greatest number of offspring.
(D) Whether a trait is harmful to the organisms of a species can depend on which sex possesses it.
(E) A trait that is helpful to procreation can also hinder it in certain environments.

2. Programmer: We computer programmers at Mytheco are demanding raises to make our average salary comparable with that of the technical writers here who receive, on average, 20 percent more in salary and benefits than we do. This pay difference is unfair and intolerable.

Mytheco executive: But many of the technical writers have worked for Mytheco longer than have many of the programmers. Since salary and benefits at Mytheco are directly tied to seniority, the 20 percent pay difference you mention is perfectly acceptable.

Evaluating the adequacy of the Mytheco executive's response requires a clarification of which one of the following?

(A) whether any of the technical writers at Mytheco once worked as programmers at the company
(B) how the average seniority of programmers compares with the average seniority of technical writers
(C) whether the sorts of benefits an employee of Mytheco receives are tied to the salary of that employee
(D) whether the Mytheco executive was at one time a technical writer employed by Mytheco
(E) how the Mytheco executive's salary compares with that of the programmers

3. Cable TV stations have advantages that enable them to attract many more advertisers than broadcast networks attract. For example, cable stations are able to target particular audiences with 24-hour news, sports, or movies, whereas broadcast networks must offer a variety of programming. Cable can also offer lower advertising rates than any broadcast network can, because it is subsidized by viewers through subscriber fees. Additionally, many cable stations have expanded worldwide with multinational programming.

The statements above, if true, provide support for each of the following EXCEPT:

(A) Some broadcast networks can be viewed in several countries.
(B) Broadcast networks do not rely on subscriber fees from viewers.
(C) Low costs are often an important factor for advertisers in selecting a station or network on which to run a TV ad.
(D) Some advertisers prefer to have the opportunity to address a worldwide audience.
(E) The audiences that some advertisers prefer to target watch 24-hour news stations.

4. In polluted industrial English cities during the Industrial Revolution, two plant diseases—black spot, which infects roses, and tar spot, which infects sycamore trees—disappeared. It is likely that air pollution eradicated these diseases.

Which one of the following, if true, most strengthens the reasoning above?

(A) Scientists theorize that some plants can develop a resistance to air pollution.
(B) Certain measures help prevent infection by black spot and tar spot, but once infection occurs, it is very difficult to eliminate.
(C) For many plant species, scientists have not determined the effects of air pollution.
(D) Black spot and tar spot returned when the air in the cities became less polluted.
(E) Black spot and tar spot were the only plant diseases that disappeared in any English cities during the Industrial Revolution.

GO ON TO THE NEXT PAGE.

5. Many scholars are puzzled about who created the seventeenth-century abridgment of Shakespeare's *Hamlet* contained in the First Quarto. Two facts about the work shed light on this question. First, the person who undertook the abridgment clearly did not possess a copy of *Hamlet*. Second, the abridgment contains a very accurate rendering of the speeches of one of the characters, but a slipshod handling of all the other parts.

Which one of the following statements is most supported by the information above?

(A) The abridgment was prepared by Shakespeare.
(B) The abridgment was created to make *Hamlet* easier to produce on stage.
(C) The abridgment was produced by an actor who had played a role in *Hamlet*.
(D) The abridgement was prepared by a spectator of a performance of *Hamlet*.
(E) The abridgment was produced by an actor who was trying to improve the play.

6. Musicologist: Many critics complain of the disproportion between text and music in Handel's *da capo* arias. These texts are generally quite short and often repeated well beyond what is needed for literal understanding. Yet such criticism is refuted by noting that repetition serves a vital function: it frees the audience to focus on the music itself, which can speak to audiences whatever their language.

Which one of the following sentences best expresses the main point of the musicologist's reasoning?

(A) Handel's *da capo* arias contain a disproportionate amount of music.
(B) Handel's *da capo* arias are superior to most in their accessibility to diverse audiences.
(C) At least one frequent criticism of Handel's *da capo* arias is undeserved.
(D) At least some of Handel's *da capo* arias contain unnecessary repetitions.
(E) Most criticism of Handel's *da capo* arias is unwarranted.

7. Baxe Interiors, one of the largest interior design companies in existence, currently has a near monopoly in the corporate market. Several small design companies have won prestigious awards for their corporate work, while Baxe has won none. Nonetheless, the corporate managers who solicit design proposals will only contract with companies they believe are unlikely to go bankrupt, and they believe that only very large companies are unlikely to go bankrupt.

The statements above, if true, most strongly support which one of the following?

(A) There are other very large design companies besides Baxe, but they produce designs that are inferior to Baxe's.
(B) Baxe does not have a near monopoly in the market of any category of interior design other than corporate interiors.
(C) For the most part, designs that are produced by small companies are superior to the designs produced by Baxe.
(D) At least some of the corporate managers who solicit design proposals are unaware that there are designs that are much better than those produced by Baxe.
(E) The existence of interior designs that are superior to those produced by Baxe does not currently threaten its near monopoly in the corporate market.

GO ON TO THE NEXT PAGE.

8. The giant Chicxulub crater in Mexico provides indisputable evidence that a huge asteroid, about six miles across, struck Earth around the time many of the last dinosaur species were becoming extinct. But this catastrophe was probably not responsible for most of these extinctions. Any major asteroid strike kills many organisms in or near the region of the impact, but there is little evidence that such a strike could have a worldwide effect. Indeed, some craters even larger than the Chicxulub crater were made during times in Earth's history when there were no known extinctions.

Which one of the following, if true, would most weaken the argument?

(A) The vast majority of dinosaur species are known to have gone extinct well before the time of the asteroid impact that produced the Chicxulub crater.

(B) The size of a crater caused by an asteroid striking Earth generally depends on both the size of that asteroid and the force of its impact.

(C) Fossils have been discovered of a number of dinosaurs that clearly died as a result of the asteroid impact that produced the Chicxulub crater.

(D) There is no evidence that any other asteroid of equal size struck Earth at the same time as the asteroid that produced the Chicxulub crater.

(E) During the period immediately before the asteroid that produced the Chicxulub crater struck, most of the world's dinosaurs lived in or near the region of the asteroid's impending impact.

9. In a sample containing 1,000 peanuts from lot A and 1,000 peanuts from lot B, 50 of the peanuts from lot A were found to be infected with *Aspergillus*. Two hundred of the peanuts from lot B were found to be infected with *Aspergillus*. Therefore, infection with *Aspergillus* is more widespread in lot B than in lot A.

The reasoning in which one of the following is most similar to the reasoning in the argument above?

(A) Every one of these varied machine parts is of uniformly high quality. Therefore, the machine that we assemble from them will be of equally high quality.

(B) If a plant is carelessly treated, it is likely to develop blight. If a plant develops blight, it is likely to die. Therefore, if a plant is carelessly treated, it is likely to die.

(C) In the past 1,000 experiments, whenever an experimental fungicide was applied to coffee plants infected with coffee rust, the infection disappeared. The coffee rust never disappeared before the fungicide was applied. Therefore, in these experiments, application of the fungicide caused the disappearance of coffee rust.

(D) Three thousand registered voters—1,500 members of the Liberal party and 1,500 members of the Conservative party—were asked which mayoral candidate they favored. Four hundred of the Liberals and 300 of the Conservatives favored Pollack. Therefore, Pollack has more support among Liberals than among Conservatives.

(E) All of my livestock are registered with the regional authority. None of the livestock registered with the regional authority are free-range livestock. Therefore, none of my livestock are free-range livestock.

GO ON TO THE NEXT PAGE.

10. Economist: If the belief were to become widespread that losing one's job is not a sign of personal shortcomings but instead an effect of impersonal social forces (which is surely correct), there would be growth in the societal demand for more government control of the economy to protect individuals from these forces, just as the government now protects them from military invasion. Such extensive government control of the economy would lead to an economic disaster, however.

The economist's statements, if true, most strongly support which one of the following?

(A) Increased knowledge of the causes of job loss could lead to economic disaster.
(B) An individual's belief in his or her own abilities is the only reliable protection against impersonal social forces.
(C) Governments should never interfere with economic forces.
(D) Societal demand for government control of the economy is growing.
(E) In general, people should feel no more responsible for economic disasters than for military invasions.

11. A development company has proposed building an airport near the city of Dalton. If the majority of Dalton's residents favor the proposal, the airport will be built. However, it is unlikely that a majority of Dalton's residents would favor the proposal, for most of them believe that the airport would create noise problems. Thus, it is unlikely that the airport will be built.

The reasoning in the argument is flawed in that the argument

(A) treats a sufficient condition for the airport's being built as a necessary condition
(B) concludes that something must be true, because most people believe it to be true
(C) concludes, on the basis that a certain event is unlikely to occur, that the event will not occur
(D) fails to consider whether people living near Dalton would favor building the airport
(E) overlooks the possibility that a new airport could benefit the local economy

12. After the rush-hour speed limit on the British M25 motorway was lowered from 70 miles per hour (115 kilometers per hour) to 50 miles per hour (80 kilometers per hour), rush-hour travel times decreased by approximately 15 percent.

Which one of the following, if true, most helps to explain the decrease in travel times described above?

(A) After the decrease in the rush-hour speed limit, the average speed on the M25 was significantly lower during rush hours than at other times of the day.
(B) Travel times during periods other than rush hours were essentially unchanged after the rush-hour speed limit was lowered.
(C) Before the rush-hour speed limit was lowered, rush-hour accidents that caused lengthy delays were common, and most of these accidents were caused by high-speed driving.
(D) Enforcement of speed limits on the M25 was quite rigorous both before and after the rush-hour speed limit was lowered.
(E) The number of people who drive on the M25 during rush hours did not increase after the rush-hour speed limit was lowered.

13. An art critic, by ridiculing an artwork, can undermine the pleasure one takes in it; conversely, by lavishing praise upon an artwork, an art critic can render the experience of viewing the artwork more pleasurable. So an artwork's artistic merit can depend not only on the person who creates it but also on those who critically evaluate it.

The conclusion can be properly drawn if which one of the following is assumed?

(A) The merit of an artistic work is determined by the amount of pleasure it elicits.
(B) Most people lack the confidence necessary for making their own evaluations of art.
(C) Art critics understand what gives an artwork artistic merit better than artists do.
(D) Most people seek out critical reviews of particular artworks before viewing those works.
(E) The pleasure people take in something is typically influenced by what they think others feel about it.

GO ON TO THE NEXT PAGE.

14. The number of automobile thefts has declined steadily during the past five years, and it is more likely now than it was five years ago that someone who steals a car will be convicted of the crime.

Which one of the following, if true, most helps to explain the facts cited above?

(A) Although there are fewer car thieves now than there were five years ago, the proportion of thieves who tend to abandon cars before their owners notice that they have been stolen has also decreased.

(B) Car alarms are more common than they were five years ago, but their propensity to be triggered in the absence of any criminal activity has resulted in people generally ignoring them when they are triggered.

(C) An upsurge in home burglaries over the last five years has required police departments to divert limited resources to investigation of these cases.

(D) Because of the increasingly lucrative market for stolen automobile parts, many stolen cars are quickly disassembled and the parts are sold to various buyers across the country.

(E) There are more adolescent car thieves now than there were five years ago, and the sentences given to young criminals tend to be far more lenient than those given to adult criminals.

15. Legislator: My staff conducted a poll in which my constituents were asked whether they favor high taxes. More than 97 percent answered "no." Clearly, then, my constituents would support the bill I recently introduced, which reduces the corporate income tax.

The reasoning in the legislator's argument is most vulnerable to criticism on the grounds that the argument

(A) fails to establish that the opinions of the legislator's constituents are representative of the opinions of the country's population as a whole

(B) fails to consider whether the legislator's constituents consider the current corporate income tax a high tax

(C) confuses an absence of evidence that the legislator's constituents oppose a bill with the existence of evidence that the legislator's constituents support that bill

(D) draws a conclusion that merely restates a claim presented in support of that conclusion

(E) treats a result that proves that the public supports a bill as a result that is merely consistent with public support for that bill

16. Many nursing homes have prohibitions against having pets, and these should be lifted. The presence of an animal companion can yield health benefits by reducing a person's stress. A pet can also make one's time at a home more rewarding, which will be important to more people as the average life span of our population increases.

Which one of the following most accurately expresses the conclusion drawn in the argument above?

(A) As the average life span increases, it will be important to more people that life in nursing homes be rewarding.

(B) Residents of nursing homes should enjoy the same rewarding aspects of life as anyone else.

(C) The policy that many nursing homes have should be changed so that residents are allowed to have pets.

(D) Having a pet can reduce one's stress and thereby make one a healthier person.

(E) The benefits older people derive from having pets need to be recognized, especially as the average life span increases.

17. Near many cities, contamination of lakes and rivers from pollutants in rainwater runoff exceeds that from industrial discharge. As the runoff washes over buildings and pavements, it picks up oil and other pollutants. Thus, water itself is among the biggest water polluters.

The statement that contamination of lakes and rivers from pollutants in rainwater runoff exceeds that from industrial discharge plays which one of the following roles in the argument?

(A) It is a conclusion for which the claim that water itself should be considered a polluter is offered as support.

(B) It is cited as evidence that pollution from rainwater runoff is a more serious problem than pollution from industrial discharge.

(C) It is a generalization based on the observation that rainwater runoff picks up oil and other pollutants as it washes over buildings and pavements.

(D) It is a premise offered in support of the conclusion that water itself is among the biggest water polluters.

(E) It is stated to provide an example of a typical kind of city pollution.

GO ON TO THE NEXT PAGE.

18. Wong: Although all countries are better off as democracies, a transitional autocratic stage is sometimes required before a country can become democratic.

Tate: The freedom and autonomy that democracy provides are of genuine value, but the simple material needs of people are more important. Some countries can better meet these needs as autocracies than as democracies.

Wong's and Tate's statements provide the most support for the claim that they disagree over the truth of which one of the following?

(A) There are some countries that are better off as autocracies than as democracies.
(B) Nothing is more important to a country than the freedom and autonomy of the individuals who live in that country.
(C) In some cases, a country cannot become a democracy.
(D) The freedom and autonomy that democracy provides are of genuine value.
(E) All democracies succeed in meeting the simple material needs of people.

19. Principle: When none of the fully qualified candidates for a new position at Arvue Corporation currently works for that company, it should hire the candidate who would be most productive in that position.

Application: Arvue should not hire Krall for the new position, because Delacruz is a candidate and is fully qualified.

Which one of the following, if true, justifies the above application of the principle?

(A) All of the candidates are fully qualified for the new position, but none already works for Arvue.
(B) Of all the candidates who do not already work for Arvue, Delacruz would be the most productive in the new position.
(C) Krall works for Arvue, but Delacruz is the candidate who would be most productive in the new position.
(D) Several candidates currently work for Arvue, but Krall and Delacruz do not.
(E) None of the candidates already works for Arvue, and Delacruz is the candidate who would be most productive in the new position.

20. Many important types of medicine have been developed from substances discovered in plants that grow only in tropical rain forests. There are thousands of plant species in these rain forests that have not yet been studied by scientists, and it is very likely that many such plants also contain substances of medicinal value. Thus, if the tropical rain forests are not preserved, important types of medicine will never be developed.

Which one of the following is an assumption required by the argument?

(A) There are substances of medicinal value contained in tropical rain forest plants not yet studied by scientists that differ from those substances already discovered in tropical rain forest plants.
(B) Most of the tropical rain forest plants that contain substances of medicinal value can also be found growing in other types of environment.
(C) The majority of plant species that are unique to tropical rain forests and that have been studied by scientists have been discovered to contain substances of medicinal value.
(D) Any substance of medicinal value contained in plant species indigenous to tropical rain forests will eventually be discovered if those species are studied by scientists.
(E) The tropical rain forests should be preserved to make it possible for important medicines to be developed from plant species that have not yet been studied by scientists.

GO ON TO THE NEXT PAGE.

21. In modern deep-diving marine mammals, such as whales, the outer shell of the bones is porous. This has the effect of making the bones light enough so that it is easy for the animals to swim back to the surface after a deep dive. The outer shell of the bones was also porous in the ichthyosaur, an extinct prehistoric marine reptile. We can conclude from this that ichthyosaurs were deep divers.

Which one of the following, if true, most weakens the argument?

(A) Some deep-diving marine species must surface after dives but do not have bones with porous outer shells.

(B) In most modern marine reptile species, the outer shell of the bones is not porous.

(C) In most modern and prehistoric marine reptile species that are not deep divers, the outer shell of the bones is porous.

(D) In addition to the porous outer shells of their bones, whales have at least some characteristics suited to deep diving for which there is no clear evidence whether these were shared by ichthyosaurs.

(E) There is evidence that the bones of ichthyosaurs would have been light enough to allow surfacing even if the outer shells were not porous.

22. Librarian: Some argue that the preservation grant we received should be used to restore our original copy of our town's charter, since if the charter is not restored, it will soon deteriorate beyond repair. But this document, although sentimentally important, has no scholarly value. Copies are readily available. Since we are a research library and not a museum, the money would be better spent preserving documents that have significant scholarly value.

The claim that the town's charter, if not restored, will soon deteriorate beyond repair plays which one of the following roles in the librarian's argument?

(A) It is a claim that the librarian's argument attempts to show to be false.

(B) It is the conclusion of the argument that the librarian's argument rejects.

(C) It is a premise in an argument whose conclusion is rejected by the librarian's argument.

(D) It is a premise used to support the librarian's main conclusion.

(E) It is a claim whose truth is required by the librarian's argument.

23. Columnist: Although much has been learned, we are still largely ignorant of the intricate interrelationships among species of living organisms. We should, therefore, try to preserve the maximum number of species if we have an interest in preserving any, since allowing species toward which we are indifferent to perish might undermine the viability of other species.

Which one of the following principles, if valid, most helps to justify the columnist's argument?

(A) It is strongly in our interest to preserve certain plant and animal species.

(B) We should not take any action until all relevant scientific facts have been established and taken into account.

(C) We should not allow the number of species to diminish any further than is necessary for the flourishing of present and future human populations.

(D) We should not allow a change to occur unless we are assured that that change will not jeopardize anything that is important to us.

(E) We should always undertake the course of action that is likely to have the best consequences in the immediate future.

24. One is likely to feel comfortable approaching a stranger if the stranger is of one's approximate age. Therefore, long-term friends are probably of the same approximate age as each other since most long-term friendships begin because someone felt comfortable approaching a stranger.

The reasoning in the argument is flawed in that it

(A) presumes, without warrant, that one is likely to feel uncomfortable approaching a person only if that person is a stranger

(B) infers that a characteristic is present in a situation from the fact that that characteristic is present in most similar situations

(C) overlooks the possibility that one is less likely to feel comfortable approaching someone who is one's approximate age if that person is a stranger than if that person is not a stranger

(D) presumes, without warrant, that one never approaches a stranger unless one feels comfortable doing so

(E) fails to address whether one is likely to feel comfortable approaching a stranger who is not one's approximate age

GO ON TO THE NEXT PAGE.

25. There can be no individual freedom without the rule of law, for there is no individual freedom without social integrity, and pursuing the good life is not possible without social integrity.

The conclusion drawn above follows logically if which one of the following is assumed?

(A) There can be no rule of law without social integrity.
(B) There can be no social integrity without the rule of law.
(C) One cannot pursue the good life without the rule of law.
(D) Social integrity is possible only if individual freedom prevails.
(E) There can be no rule of law without individual freedom.

26. Economist: Countries with an uneducated population are destined to be weak economically and politically, whereas those with an educated population have governments that display a serious financial commitment to public education. So any nation with a government that has made such a commitment will avoid economic and political weakness.

The pattern of flawed reasoning in which one of the following arguments is most similar to that in the economist's argument?

(A) Animal species with a very narrow diet will have more difficulty surviving if the climate suddenly changes, but a species with a broader diet will not; for changes in the climate can remove the traditional food supply.
(B) People incapable of empathy are not good candidates for public office, but those who do have the capacity for empathy are able to manipulate others easily; hence, people who can manipulate others are good candidates for public office.
(C) People who cannot give orders are those who do not understand the personalities of the people to whom they give orders. Thus, those who can give orders are those who understand the personalities of the people to whom they give orders.
(D) Poets who create poetry of high quality are those who have studied traditional poetry, because poets who have not studied traditional poetry are the poets most likely to create something shockingly inventive, and poetry that is shockingly inventive is rarely fine poetry.
(E) People who dislike exercise are unlikely to lose weight without sharply curtailing their food intake; but since those who dislike activity generally tend to avoid it, people who like to eat but dislike exercise will probably fail to lose weight.

STOP
IF YOU FINISH BEFORE TIME IS CALLED, YOU MAY CHECK YOUR WORK ON THIS SECTION ONLY.
DO NOT WORK ON ANY OTHER SECTION IN THE TEST.

ACKNOWLEDGMENTS

Acknowledgment is made to the following sources from which material has been adapted for use in this test booklet:

Robin D. G. Kelley, "But a Local Phase of a World Problem: Black History's Global Vision, 1883–1950." ©1999 by the Organization of American Historians.

Alfred Lessing, "What Is Wrong With a Forgery?" in *The Forger's Art.* ©1983 by The Regents of the University of California.

David Pitts, "The Noble Endeavor: The Creation of the Universal Declaration of Human Rights." ©2001 by U.S. Department of State, Office of International Information Programs.

Ellen Rosand, "It Bears Repeating." ©1996 by Metropolitan Opera Guild, Inc.

Wait for the supervisor's instructions before you open the page to the topic.
Please print and sign your name and write the date in the designated spaces below.
Time: 35 Minutes

General Directions

You will have 35 minutes in which to plan and write an essay on the topic inside. Read the topic and the accompanying directions carefully. You will probably find it best to spend a few minutes considering the topic and organizing your thoughts before you begin writing. In your essay, be sure to develop your ideas fully, leaving time, if possible, to review what you have written. **Do not write on a topic other than the one specified. Writing on a topic of your own choice is not acceptable.**

No special knowledge is required or expected for this writing exercise. Law schools are interested in the reasoning, clarity, organization, language usage, and writing mechanics displayed in your essay. How well you write is more important than how much you write.

Confine your essay to the blocked, lined area on the front and back of the separate Writing Sample Response Sheet. Only that area will be reproduced for law schools. Be sure that your writing is legible.

Both this topic sheet and your response sheet must be turned over to the testing staff before you leave the room.

Topic Code	Print Your Full Name Here		
	Last	First	M.I.

Date	Sign Your Name Here
/ /	

Scratch Paper
Do not write your essay in this space.

LSAT® Writing Sample Topic

Directions: The scenario presented below describes two choices, either one of which can be supported on the basis of the information given. Your essay should consider both choices and argue for one over the other, based on the two specified criteria and the facts provided. There is no "right" or "wrong" choice: a reasonable argument can be made for either.

The attorneys for the plaintiffs in a lawsuit against a major pharmaceutical company are choosing an expert scientific witness to testify that a drug produced by the company was responsible for serious side effects. The attorneys have narrowed their choices down to two people. Using the facts below, write an essay in which you argue for choosing one person over the other based on the following two criteria:

- The attorneys want a witness who will be able to communicate technical information in a clear and effective manner to the jury.
- The attorneys want a witness who is highly knowledgeable in the field of pharmacology.

Dr. Rosa Benally has qualifications similar to those of the defense team's expert witness in that she has a PhD in pharmacology, teaches at a university, and is highly respected for her scientific research. Dr. Benally recently led a series of studies investigating the side effects of the class of drugs that will be under discussion during the trial. She has served effectively as an expert witness in a number of similar trials over the last five years.

Dr. Josephine Rickman is a medical doctor who also has a PhD in pharmacology. She has a busy medical practice. Dr. Rickman sometimes serves as a medical news correspondent on a national news program. She is the author of three best-selling books on medical topics, including one on the pharmaceutical industry. Dr. Rickman prescribed the drug in question to a number of patients who appeared to have experienced side effects like those to be discussed during the trial.

WP-S097A

Scratch Paper
Do not write your essay in this space.

Writing Sample Response Sheet

DO NOT WRITE
IN THIS SPACE

**Begin your essay in the lined area below.
Continue on the back if you need more space.**

COMPUTING YOUR SCORE

Directions:

1. Use the Answer Key on the next page to check your answers.

2. Use the Scoring Worksheet below to compute your raw score.

3. Use the Score Conversion Chart to convert your raw score into the 120-180 scale.

Scoring Worksheet

1. Enter the number of questions you answered correctly in each section.

	Number Correct
SECTION I	_____
SECTION II	_____
SECTION III	_____
SECTION IV..............	_____

2. Enter the sum here: _____

   This is your Raw Score.

Conversion Chart
For Converting Raw Score to the 120-180 LSAT Scaled Score
LSAT Form 0LSN86

Reported Score	Raw Score Lowest	Raw Score Highest
180	99	101
179	98	98
178	97	97
177	96	96
176	—*	—*
175	95	95
174	94	94
173	93	93
172	92	92
171	91	91
170	89	90
169	88	88
168	87	87
167	85	86
166	84	84
165	82	83
164	81	81
163	79	80
162	78	78
161	76	77
160	74	75
159	73	73
158	71	72
157	69	70
156	67	68
155	66	66
154	64	65
153	62	63
152	60	61
151	58	59
150	57	57
149	55	56
148	53	54
147	52	52
146	50	51
145	48	49
144	47	47
143	45	46
142	43	44
141	42	42
140	40	41
139	39	39
138	37	38
137	36	36
136	34	35
135	33	33
134	31	32
133	30	30
132	29	29
131	27	28
130	26	26
129	25	25
128	24	24
127	22	23
126	21	21
125	20	20
124	19	19
123	18	18
122	16	17
121	—*	—*
120	0	15

*There is no raw score that will produce this scaled score for this form.

ANSWER KEY

SECTION I

1.	D	8.	A	15.	A	22.	A
2.	B	9.	E	16.	D	23.	E
3.	B	10.	C	17.	D	24.	E
4.	D	11.	B	18.	C	25.	B
5.	E	12.	E	19.	B	26.	A
6.	A	13.	B	20.	D	27.	B
7.	C	14.	B	21.	E		

SECTION II

1.	D	8.	A	15.	B	22.	C
2.	E	9.	E	16.	C	23.	D
3.	C	10.	A	17.	A	24.	B
4.	D	11.	A	18.	A	25.	D
5.	A	12.	A	19.	D		
6.	C	13.	B	20.	C		
7.	D	14.	D	21.	E		

SECTION III

1.	A	8.	A	15.	A	22.	B
2.	E	9.	C	16.	E	23.	A
3.	A	10.	B	17.	B		
4.	C	11.	D	18.	D		
5.	D	12.	D	19.	C		
6.	A	13.	D	20.	D		
7.	C	14.	B	21.	B		

SECTION IV

1.	E	8.	E	15.	B	22.	C
2.	B	9.	D	16.	C	23.	D
3.	A	10.	A	17.	D	24.	E
4.	D	11.	A	18.	A	25.	B
5.	C	12.	C	19.	E	26.	B
6.	C	13.	A	20.	A		
7.	E	14.	A	21.	C		

PREPTEST 62
DECEMBER 2010
FORM 0LSN85

SECTION I

Time—35 minutes

27 Questions

<u>Directions:</u> Each set of questions in this section is based on a single passage or a pair of passages. The questions are to be answered on the basis of what is <u>stated</u> or <u>implied</u> in the passage or pair of passages. For some of the questions, more than one of the choices could conceivably answer the question. However, you are to choose the <u>best</u> answer; that is, the response that most accurately and completely answers the question, and blacken the corresponding space on your answer sheet.

To study centuries-old earthquakes and the geologic faults that caused them, seismologists usually dig trenches along visible fault lines, looking for sediments that show evidence of having shifted. Using radiocarbon
(5) dating, they measure the quantity of the radioactive isotope carbon 14 present in wood or other organic material trapped in the sediments when they shifted. Since carbon 14 occurs naturally in organic materials and decays at a constant rate, the age of organic
(10) materials can be reconstructed from the amount of the isotope remaining in them. These data can show the location and frequency of past earthquakes and provide hints about the likelihood and location of future earthquakes.
(15) Geologists William Bull and Mark Brandon have recently developed a new method, called lichenometry, for detecting and dating past earthquakes. Bull and Brandon developed the method based on the fact that large earthquakes generate numerous simultaneous
(20) rockfalls in mountain ranges that are sensitive to seismic shaking. Instead of dating fault-line sediments, lichenometry involves measuring the size of lichens growing on the rocks exposed by these rockfalls. Lichens—symbiotic organisms consisting of a fungus
(25) and an alga—quickly colonize newly exposed rock surfaces in the wake of rockfalls, and once established they grow radially, flat against the rocks, at a slow but constant rate for as long as 1,000 years if left undisturbed. One species of North American lichen, for example,
(30) spreads outward by about 9.5 millimeters each century. Hence, the diameter of the largest lichen on a boulder provides direct evidence of when the boulder was dislodged and repositioned. If many rockfalls over a large geographic area occurred simultaneously, that
(35) pattern would imply that there had been a strong earthquake. The location of the earthquake's epicenter can then be determined by mapping these rockfalls, since they decrease in abundance as the distance from the epicenter increases.
(40) Lichenometry has distinct advantages over radiocarbon dating. Radiocarbon dating is accurate only to within plus or minus 40 years, because the amount of the carbon 14 isotope varies naturally in the environment depending on the intensity of the radiation
(45) striking Earth's upper atmosphere. Additionally, this intensity has fluctuated greatly during the past 300 years, causing many radiocarbon datings of events during this period to be of little value. Lichenometry, Bull and Brandon claim, can accurately date an
(50) earthquake to within ten years. They note, however, that using lichenometry requires careful site selection

and accurate calibration of lichen growth rates, adding that the method is best used for earthquakes that occurred within the last 500 years. Sites must be selected to minimize the influence of snow avalanches
(55) and other disturbances that would affect normal lichen growth, and conditions like shade and wind that promote faster lichen growth must be factored in.

1. Which one of the following most accurately expresses the main idea of the passage?

(A) Lichenometry is a new method for dating past earthquakes that has advantages over radiocarbon dating.

(B) Despite its limitations, lichenometry has been proven to be more accurate than any other method of discerning the dates of past earthquakes.

(C) Most seismologists today have rejected radiocarbon dating and are embracing lichenometry as the most reliable method for studying past earthquakes.

(D) Two geologists have revolutionized the study of past earthquakes by developing lichenometry, an easily applied method of earthquake detection and dating.

(E) Radiocarbon dating, an unreliable test used in dating past earthquakes, can finally be abandoned now that lichenometry has been developed.

2. The passage provides information that most helps to answer which one of the following questions?

(A) How do scientists measure lichen growth rates under the varying conditions that lichens may encounter?

(B) How do scientists determine the intensity of the radiation striking Earth's upper atmosphere?

(C) What are some of the conditions that encourage lichens to grow at a more rapid rate than usual?

(D) What is the approximate date of the earliest earthquake that lichenometry has been used to identify?

(E) What are some applications of the techniques involved in radiocarbon dating other than their use in studying past earthquakes?

GO ON TO THE NEXT PAGE.

3. What is the author's primary purpose in referring to the rate of growth of a North American lichen species (lines 29–30)?

(A) to emphasize the rapidity with which lichen colonies can establish themselves on newly exposed rock surfaces

(B) to offer an example of a lichen species with one of the slowest known rates of growth

(C) to present additional evidence supporting the claim that environmental conditions can alter lichens' rate of growth

(D) to explain why lichenometry works best for dating earthquakes that occurred in the last 500 years

(E) to provide a sense of the sort of timescale on which lichen growth occurs

4. Which one of the following statements is most strongly supported by the passage?

(A) Lichenometry is less accurate than radiocarbon dating in predicting the likelihood and location of future earthquakes.

(B) Radiocarbon dating is unlikely to be helpful in dating past earthquakes that have no identifiable fault lines associated with them.

(C) Radiocarbon dating and lichenometry are currently the only viable methods of detecting and dating past earthquakes.

(D) Radiocarbon dating is more accurate than lichenometry in dating earthquakes that occurred approximately 400 years ago.

(E) The usefulness of lichenometry for dating earthquakes is limited to geographic regions where factors that disturb or accelerate lichen growth generally do not occur.

5. The primary purpose of the first paragraph in relation to the rest of the passage is to describe

(A) a well-known procedure that will then be examined on a step-by-step basis

(B) an established procedure to which a new procedure will then be compared

(C) an outdated procedure that will then be shown to be nonetheless useful in some situations

(D) a traditional procedure that will then be contrasted with other traditional procedures

(E) a popular procedure that will then be shown to have resulted in erroneous conclusions about a phenomenon

6. It can be inferred that the statements made by Bull and Brandon and reported in lines 50–58 rely on which one of the following assumptions?

(A) While lichenometry is less accurate when it is used to date earthquakes that occurred more than 500 years ago, it is still more accurate than other methods for dating such earthquakes.

(B) There is no reliable method for determining the intensity of the radiation now hitting Earth's upper atmosphere.

(C) Lichens are able to grow only on the types of rocks that are common in mountainous regions.

(D) The mountain ranges that produce the kinds of rockfalls studied in lichenometry are also subject to more frequent snowfalls and avalanches than other mountain ranges are.

(E) The extent to which conditions like shade and wind have affected the growth of existing lichen colonies can be determined.

7. The passage indicates that using radiocarbon dating to date past earthquakes may be unreliable due to

(A) the multiplicity of the types of organic matter that require analysis

(B) the variable amount of organic materials caught in shifted sediments

(C) the fact that fault lines related to past earthquakes are not always visible

(D) the fluctuations in the amount of the carbon 14 isotope in the environment over time

(E) the possibility that radiation has not always struck the upper atmosphere

8. Given the information in the passage, to which one of the following would lichenometry likely be most applicable?

(A) identifying the number of times a particular river has flooded in the past 1,000 years

(B) identifying the age of a fossilized skeleton of a mammal that lived many thousands of years ago

(C) identifying the age of an ancient beach now underwater approximately 30 kilometers off the present shore

(D) identifying the rate, in kilometers per century, at which a glacier has been receding up a mountain valley

(E) identifying local trends in annual rainfall rates in a particular valley over the past five centuries

GO ON TO THE NEXT PAGE.

While courts have long allowed custom-made medical illustrations depicting personal injury to be presented as evidence in legal cases, the issue of whether they have a legitimate place in the courtroom
(5) is surrounded by ongoing debate and misinformation. Some opponents of their general use argue that while illustrations are sometimes invaluable in presenting the physical details of a personal injury, in all cases except those involving the most unusual injuries, illustrations
(10) from medical textbooks can be adequate. Most injuries, such as fractures and whiplash, they say, are rather generic in nature—certain commonly encountered forces act on particular areas of the body in standard ways—so they can be represented by
(15) generic illustrations.

Another line of complaint stems from the belief that custom-made illustrations often misrepresent the facts in order to comply with the partisan interests of litigants. Even some lawyers appear to share a version
(20) of this view, believing that such illustrations can be used to bolster a weak case. Illustrators are sometimes approached by lawyers who, unable to find medical experts to support their clients' claims, think that they can replace expert testimony with such deceptive
(25) professional illustrations. But this is mistaken. Even if an unscrupulous illustrator could be found, such illustrations would be inadmissible as evidence in the courtroom unless a medical expert were present to testify to their accuracy.

(30) It has also been maintained that custom-made illustrations may subtly distort the issues through the use of emphasis, coloration, and other means, even if they are technically accurate. But professional medical illustrators strive for objective accuracy and avoid
(35) devices that have inflammatory potential, sometimes even eschewing the use of color. Unlike illustrations in medical textbooks, which are designed to include the extensive detail required by medical students, custom-made medical illustrations are designed to
(40) include only the information that is relevant for those deciding a case. The end user is typically a jury or a judge, for whose benefit the depiction is reduced to the details that are crucial to determining the legally relevant facts. The more complex details often found
(45) in textbooks can be deleted so as not to confuse the issue. For example, illustrations of such things as veins and arteries would only get in the way when an illustration is supposed to be used to explain the nature of a bone fracture.

(50) Custom-made medical illustrations, which are based on a plaintiff's X rays, computerized tomography scans, and medical records and reports, are especially valuable in that they provide visual representations of data whose verbal description would
(55) be very complex. Expert testimony by medical professionals often relies heavily on the use of technical terminology, which those who are not

specially trained in the field find difficult to translate mentally into visual imagery. Since, for most people,
(60) adequate understanding of physical data depends on thinking at least partly in visual terms, the clearly presented visual stimulation provided by custom-made illustrations can be quite instructive.

9. Which one of the following is most analogous to the role that, according to the author, custom-made medical illustrations play in personal injury cases?

(A) schematic drawings accompanying an engineer's oral presentation
(B) road maps used by people unfamiliar with an area so that they will not have to get verbal instructions from strangers
(C) children's drawings that psychologists use to detect wishes and anxieties not apparent in the children's behavior
(D) a reproduction of a famous painting in an art history textbook
(E) an artist's preliminary sketches for a painting

10. Based on the passage, which one of the following is the author most likely to believe about illustrations in medical textbooks?

(A) They tend to rely less on the use of color than do custom-made medical illustrations.
(B) They are inadmissible in a courtroom unless a medical expert is present to testify to their accuracy.
(C) They are in many cases drawn by the same individuals who draw custom-made medical illustrations for courtroom use.
(D) They are believed by most lawyers to be less prone than custom-made medical illustrations to misrepresent the nature of a personal injury.
(E) In many cases they are more apt to confuse jurors than are custom-made medical illustrations.

11. The passage states that a role of medical experts in relation to custom-made medical illustrations in the courtroom is to

(A) decide which custom-made medical illustrations should be admissible
(B) temper the impact of the illustrations on judges and jurors who are not medical professionals
(C) make medical illustrations understandable to judges and jurors
(D) provide opinions to attorneys as to which illustrations, if any, would be useful
(E) provide their opinions as to the accuracy of the illustrations

GO ON TO THE NEXT PAGE.

12. According to the passage, one of the ways that medical textbook illustrations differ from custom-made medical illustrations is that

(A) custom-made medical illustrations accurately represent human anatomy, whereas medical textbook illustrations do not

(B) medical textbook illustrations employ color freely, whereas custom-made medical illustrations must avoid color

(C) medical textbook illustrations are objective, while custom-made medical illustrations are subjective

(D) medical textbook illustrations are very detailed, whereas custom-made medical illustrations include only details that are relevant to the case

(E) medical textbook illustrations are readily comprehended by nonmedical audiences, whereas custom-made medical illustrations are not

13. The author's attitude toward the testimony of medical experts in personal injury cases is most accurately described as

(A) appreciation of the difficulty involved in explaining medical data to judges and jurors together with skepticism concerning the effectiveness of such testimony

(B) admiration for the experts' technical knowledge coupled with disdain for the communications skills of medical professionals

(C) acceptance of the accuracy of such testimony accompanied with awareness of the limitations of a presentation that is entirely verbal

(D) respect for the medical profession tempered by apprehension concerning the tendency of medical professionals to try to overwhelm judges and jurors with technical details

(E) respect for expert witnesses combined with intolerance of the use of technical terminology

14. The author's primary purpose in the third paragraph is to

(A) argue for a greater use of custom-made medical illustrations in court cases involving personal injury

(B) reply to a variant of the objection to custom-made medical illustrations raised in the second paragraph

(C) argue against the position that illustrations from medical textbooks are well suited for use in the courtroom

(D) discuss in greater detail why custom-made medical illustrations are controversial

(E) describe the differences between custom-made medical illustrations and illustrations from medical textbooks

GO ON TO THE NEXT PAGE.

Passage A

Because dental caries (decay) is strongly linked to consumption of the sticky, carbohydrate-rich staples of agricultural diets, prehistoric human teeth can provide clues about when a population made the transition
(5) from a hunter-gatherer diet to an agricultural one. Caries formation is influenced by several factors, including tooth structure, bacteria in the mouth, and diet. In particular, caries formation is affected by carbohydrates' texture and composition, since
(10) carbohydrates more readily stick to teeth.

Many researchers have demonstrated the link between carbohydrate consumption and caries. In North America, Leigh studied caries in archaeologically derived teeth, noting that caries rates differed between
(15) indigenous populations that primarily consumed meat (a Sioux sample showed almost no caries) and those heavily dependent on cultivated maize (a Zuni sample had 75 percent carious teeth). Leigh's findings have been frequently confirmed by other researchers, who
(20) have shown that, in general, the greater a population's dependence on agriculture is, the higher its rate of caries formation will be.

Under some circumstances, however, nonagricultural populations may exhibit relatively
(25) high caries rates. For example, early nonagricultural populations in western North America who consumed large amounts of highly processed stone-ground flour made from gathered acorns show relatively high caries frequencies. And wild plants collected by the Hopi
(30) included several species with high cariogenic potential, notably pinyon nuts and wild tubers.

Passage B

Archaeologists recovered human skeletal remains interred over a 2,000-year period in prehistoric Ban Chiang, Thailand. The site's early inhabitants
(35) appear to have had a hunter-gatherer-cultivator economy. Evidence indicates that, over time, the population became increasingly dependent on agriculture.

Research suggests that agricultural intensification
(40) results in declining human health, including dental health. Studies show that dental caries is uncommon in pre-agricultural populations. Increased caries frequency may result from increased consumption of starchy-sticky foodstuffs or from alterations in tooth wear. The
(45) wearing down of tooth crown surfaces reduces caries formation by removing fissures that can trap food particles. A reduction of fiber or grit in a diet may diminish tooth wear, thus increasing caries frequency. However, severe wear that exposes a tooth's pulp
(50) cavity may also result in caries.

The diet of Ban Chiang's inhabitants included some cultivated rice and yams from the beginning of the period represented by the recovered remains. These were part of a varied diet that also included
(55) wild plant and animal foods. Since both rice and yams are carbohydrates, increased reliance on either or both should theoretically result in increased caries frequency.

Yet comparisons of caries frequency in the Early and Late Ban Chiang Groups indicate that overall
(60) caries frequency is slightly greater in the Early Group. Tooth wear patterns do not indicate tooth wear changes between Early and Late Groups that would explain this unexpected finding. It is more likely that, although dependence on agriculture increased, the diet
(65) in the Late period remained varied enough that no single food dominated. Furthermore, there may have been a shift from sweeter carbohydrates (yams) toward rice, a less cariogenic carbohydrate.

15. Both passages are primarily concerned with examining which one of the following topics?

(A) evidence of the development of agriculture in the archaeological record
(B) the impact of agriculture on the overall health of human populations
(C) the effects of carbohydrate-rich foods on caries formation in strictly agricultural societies
(D) the archaeological evidence regarding when the first agricultural society arose
(E) the extent to which pre-agricultural populations were able to obtain carbohydrate-rich foods

16. Which one of the following distinguishes the Ban Chiang populations discussed in passage B from the populations discussed in the last paragraph of passage A?

(A) While the Ban Chiang populations consumed several highly cariogenic foods, the populations discussed in the last paragraph of passage A did not.
(B) While the Ban Chiang populations ate cultivated foods, the populations discussed in the last paragraph of passage A did not.
(C) While the Ban Chiang populations consumed a diet consisting primarily of carbohydrates, the populations discussed in the last paragraph of passage A did not.
(D) While the Ban Chiang populations exhibited very high levels of tooth wear, the populations discussed in the last paragraph of passage A did not.
(E) While the Ban Chiang populations ate certain highly processed foods, the populations discussed in the last paragraph of passage A did not.

GO ON TO THE NEXT PAGE.

17. Passage B most strongly supports which one of the following statements about fiber and grit in a diet?

(A) They can either limit or promote caries formation, depending on their prevalence in the diet.
(B) They are typically consumed in greater quantities as a population adopts agriculture.
(C) They have a negative effect on overall health since they have no nutritional value.
(D) They contribute to the formation of fissures in tooth surfaces.
(E) They increase the stickiness of carbohydrate-rich foods.

18. Which one of the following is mentioned in both passages as evidence tending to support the prevailing view regarding the relationship between dental caries and carbohydrate consumption?

(A) the effect of consuming highly processed foods on caries formation
(B) the relatively low incidence of caries among nonagricultural people
(C) the effect of fiber and grit in the diet on caries formation
(D) the effect of the consumption of wild foods on tooth wear
(E) the effect of agricultural intensification on overall human health

19. It is most likely that both authors would agree with which one of the following statements about dental caries?

(A) The incidence of dental caries increases predictably in populations over time.
(B) Dental caries is often difficult to detect in teeth recovered from archaeological sites.
(C) Dental caries tends to be more prevalent in populations with a hunter-gatherer diet than in populations with an agricultural diet.
(D) The frequency of dental caries in a population does not necessarily correspond directly to the population's degree of dependence on agriculture.
(E) The formation of dental caries tends to be more strongly linked to tooth wear than to the consumption of a particular kind of food.

20. Each passage suggests which one of the following about carbohydrate-rich foods?

(A) Varieties that are cultivated have a greater tendency to cause caries than varieties that grow wild.
(B) Those that require substantial processing do not play a role in hunter-gatherer diets.
(C) Some of them naturally have a greater tendency than others to cause caries.
(D) Some of them reduce caries formation because their relatively high fiber content increases tooth wear.
(E) The cariogenic potential of a given variety increases if it is cultivated rather than gathered in the wild.

21. The evidence from Ban Chiang discussed in passage B relates to the generalization reported in the second paragraph of passage A (lines 20–22) in which one of the following ways?

(A) The evidence confirms the generalization.
(B) The evidence tends to support the generalization.
(C) The evidence is irrelevant to the generalization.
(D) The evidence does not conform to the generalization.
(E) The evidence disproves the generalization.

GO ON TO THE NEXT PAGE.

Recent criticism has sought to align Sarah Orne Jewett, a notable writer of regional fiction in the nineteenth-century United States, with the domestic novelists of the previous generation. Her work does
(5) resemble the domestic novels of the 1850s in its focus on women, their domestic occupations, and their social interactions, with men relegated to the periphery. But it also differs markedly from these antecedents. The world depicted in the latter revolves around children.
(10) Young children play prominent roles in the domestic novels and the work of child rearing—the struggle to instill a mother's values in a child's character—is their chief source of drama. By contrast, children and child rearing are almost entirely absent from the world of
(15) Jewett's fiction. Even more strikingly, while the literary world of the earlier domestic novelists is insistently religious, grounded in the structures of Protestant religious belief, to turn from these writers to Jewett is to encounter an almost wholly secular world.
(20) To the extent that these differences do not merely reflect the personal preferences of the authors, we might attribute them to such historical transformations as the migration of the rural young to cities or the increasing secularization of society. But while such
(25) factors may help to explain the differences, it can be argued that these differences ultimately reflect different conceptions of the nature and purpose of fiction. The domestic novel of the mid-nineteenth century is based on a conception of fiction as part of
(30) a continuum that also included writings devoted to piety and domestic instruction, bound together by a common goal of promoting domestic morality and religious belief. It was not uncommon for the same multipurpose book to be indistinguishably a novel, a
(35) child-rearing manual, and a tract on Christian duty. The more didactic aims are absent from Jewett's writing, which rather embodies the late nineteenth-century "high-cultural" conception of fiction as an autonomous sphere with value in and of itself.
(40) This high-cultural aesthetic was one among several conceptions of fiction operative in the United States in the 1850s and 1860s, but it became the dominant one later in the nineteenth century and remained so for most of the twentieth. On this
(45) conception, fiction came to be seen as pure art: a work was to be viewed in isolation and valued for the formal arrangement of its elements rather than for its larger social connections or the promotion of extraliterary goods. Thus, unlike the domestic novelists, Jewett
(50) intended her works not as a means to an end but as an end in themselves. This fundamental difference should be given more weight in assessing their affinities than any superficial similarity in subject matter.

22. The passage most helps to answer which one of the following questions?

(A) Did any men write domestic novels in the 1850s?
(B) Were any widely read domestic novels written after the 1860s?
(C) How did migration to urban areas affect the development of domestic fiction in the 1850s?
(D) What is an effect that Jewett's conception of literary art had on her fiction?
(E) With what region of the United States were at least some of Jewett's writings concerned?

23. It can be inferred from the passage that the author would be most likely to view the "recent criticism" mentioned in line 1 as

(A) advocating a position that is essentially correct even though some powerful arguments can be made against it
(B) making a true claim about Jewett, but for the wrong reasons
(C) making a claim that is based on some reasonable evidence and is initially plausible but ultimately mistaken
(D) questionable, because it relies on a currently dominant literary aesthetic that takes too narrow a view of the proper goals of fiction
(E) based on speculation for which there is no reasonable support, and therefore worthy of dismissal

24. In saying that domestic fiction was based on a conception of fiction as part of a "continuum" (line 30), the author most likely means which one of the following?

(A) Domestic fiction was part of an ongoing tradition stretching back into the past.
(B) Fiction was not treated as clearly distinct from other categories of writing.
(C) Domestic fiction was often published in serial form.
(D) Fiction is constantly evolving.
(E) Domestic fiction promoted the cohesiveness and hence the continuity of society.

GO ON TO THE NEXT PAGE.

25. Which one of the following most accurately states the primary function of the passage?

   (A)   It proposes and defends a radical redefinition of several historical categories of literary style.
   (B)   It proposes an evaluation of a particular style of writing, of which one writer's work is cited as a paradigmatic case.
   (C)   It argues for a reappraisal of a set of long-held assumptions about the historical connections among a group of writers.
   (D)   It weighs the merits of two opposing conceptions of the nature of fiction.
   (E)   It rejects a way of classifying a particular writer's work and defends an alternative view.

26. Which one of the following most accurately represents the structure of the second paragraph?

   (A)   The author considers and rejects a number of possible explanations for a phenomenon, concluding that any attempt at explanation does violence to the unity of the phenomenon.
   (B)   The author shows that two explanatory hypotheses are incompatible with each other and gives reasons for preferring one of them.
   (C)   The author describes several explanatory hypotheses and argues that they are not really distinct from one another.
   (D)   The author proposes two versions of a classificatory hypothesis, indicates the need for some such hypothesis, and then sets out a counterargument in preparation for rejecting that counterargument in the following paragraph.
   (E)   The author mentions a number of explanatory hypotheses, gives a mildly favorable comment on them, and then advocates and elaborates another explanation that the author considers to be more fundamental.

27. The differing conceptions of fiction held by Jewett and the domestic novelists can most reasonably be taken as providing an answer to which one of the following questions?

   (A)   Why was Jewett unwilling to feature children and religious themes as prominently in her works as the domestic novelists featured them in theirs?
   (B)   Why did both Jewett and the domestic novelists focus primarily on rural as opposed to urban concerns?
   (C)   Why was Jewett not constrained to feature children and religion as prominently in her works as domestic novelists were?
   (D)   Why did both Jewett and the domestic novelists focus predominantly on women and their concerns?
   (E)   Why was Jewett unable to feature children or religion as prominently in her works as the domestic novelists featured them in theirs?

STOP
IF YOU FINISH BEFORE TIME IS CALLED, YOU MAY CHECK YOUR WORK ON THIS SECTION ONLY.
DO NOT WORK ON ANY OTHER SECTION IN THE TEST.

SECTION II

Time—35 minutes

26 Questions

Directions: The questions in this section are based on the reasoning contained in brief statements or passages. For some questions, more than one of the choices could conceivably answer the question. However, you are to choose the best answer; that is, the response that most accurately and completely answers the question. You should not make assumptions that are by commonsense standards implausible, superfluous, or incompatible with the passage. After you have chosen the best answer, blacken the corresponding space on your answer sheet.

1. In a recent study, a group of young children were taught the word "stairs" while walking up and down a flight of stairs. Later that day, when the children were shown a video of a person climbing a ladder, they all called the ladder stairs.

   Which one of the following principles is best illustrated by the study described above?

   (A) When young children repeatedly hear a word without seeing the object denoted by the word, they sometimes apply the word to objects not denoted by the word.

   (B) Young children best learn words when they are shown how the object denoted by the word is used.

   (C) The earlier in life a child encounters and uses an object, the easier it is for that child to learn how not to misuse the word denoting that object.

   (D) Young children who learn a word by observing how the object denoted by that word is used sometimes apply that word to a different object that is similarly used.

   (E) Young children best learn the names of objects when the objects are present at the time the children learn the words and when no other objects are simultaneously present.

2. Among people who live to the age of 100 or more, a large proportion have led "unhealthy" lives: smoking, consuming alcohol, eating fatty foods, and getting little exercise. Since such behavior often leads to shortened life spans, it is likely that exceptionally long-lived people are genetically disposed to having long lives.

   Which one of the following, if true, most strengthens the argument?

   (A) There is some evidence that consuming a moderate amount of alcohol can counteract the effects of eating fatty foods.

   (B) Some of the exceptionally long-lived people who do not smoke or drink do eat fatty foods and get little exercise.

   (C) Some of the exceptionally long-lived people who exercise regularly and avoid fatty foods do smoke or consume alcohol.

   (D) Some people who do not live to the age of 100 also lead unhealthy lives.

   (E) Nearly all people who live to 100 or more have siblings who are also long-lived.

3. Medications with an unpleasant taste are generally produced only in tablet, capsule, or soft-gel form. The active ingredient in medication M is a waxy substance that cannot tolerate the heat used to manufacture tablets because it has a low melting point. So, since the company developing M does not have soft-gel manufacturing technology and manufactures all its medications itself, M will most likely be produced in capsule form.

   The conclusion is most strongly supported by the reasoning in the argument if which one of the following is assumed?

   (A) Medication M can be produced in liquid form.

   (B) Medication M has an unpleasant taste.

   (C) No medication is produced in both capsule and soft-gel form.

   (D) Most medications with a low melting point are produced in soft-gel form.

   (E) Medications in capsule form taste less unpleasant than those in tablet or soft-gel form.

GO ON TO THE NEXT PAGE.

4. Carol Morris wants to own a majority of the shares of the city's largest newspaper, *The Daily*. The only obstacle to Morris's amassing a majority of these shares is that Azedcorp, which currently owns a majority, has steadfastly refused to sell. Industry analysts nevertheless predict that Morris will soon be the majority owner of *The Daily*.

Which one of the following, if true, provides the most support for the industry analysts' prediction?

(A) Azedcorp does not own shares of any newspaper other than *The Daily*.

(B) Morris has recently offered Azedcorp much more for its shares of *The Daily* than Azedcorp paid for them.

(C) No one other than Morris has expressed any interest in purchasing a majority of *The Daily*'s shares.

(D) Morris already owns more shares of *The Daily* than anyone except Azedcorp.

(E) Azedcorp is financially so weak that bankruptcy will probably soon force the sale of its newspaper holdings.

5. Area resident: Childhood lead poisoning has declined steadily since the 1970s, when leaded gasoline was phased out and lead paint was banned. But recent statistics indicate that 25 percent of this area's homes still contain lead paint that poses significant health hazards. Therefore, if we eliminate the lead paint in those homes, childhood lead poisoning in the area will finally be eradicated.

The area resident's argument is flawed in that it

(A) relies on statistical claims that are likely to be unreliable

(B) relies on an assumption that is tantamount to assuming that the conclusion is true

(C) fails to consider that there may be other significant sources of lead in the area's environment

(D) takes for granted that lead paint in homes can be eliminated economically

(E) takes for granted that children reside in all of the homes in the area that contain lead paint

6. Although some nutritional facts about soft drinks are listed on their labels, exact caffeine content is not. Listing exact caffeine content would make it easier to limit, but not eliminate, one's caffeine intake. If it became easier for people to limit, but not eliminate, their caffeine intake, many people would do so, which would improve their health.

If all the statements above are true, which one of the following must be true?

(A) The health of at least some people would improve if exact caffeine content were listed on soft-drink labels.

(B) Many people will be unable to limit their caffeine intake if exact caffeine content is not listed on soft-drink labels.

(C) Many people will find it difficult to eliminate their caffeine intake if they have to guess exactly how much caffeine is in their soft drinks.

(D) People who wish to eliminate, rather than simply limit, their caffeine intake would benefit if exact caffeine content were listed on soft-drink labels.

(E) The health of at least some people would worsen if everyone knew exactly how much caffeine was in their soft drinks.

7. When the famous art collector Vidmar died, a public auction of her collection, the largest privately owned, was held. "I can't possibly afford any of those works because hers is among the most valuable collections ever assembled by a single person," declared art lover MacNeil.

The flawed pattern of reasoning in which one of the following is most closely parallel to that in MacNeil's argument?

(A) Each word in the book is in French. So the whole book is in French.

(B) The city council voted unanimously to adopt the plan. So councilperson Martinez voted to adopt the plan.

(C) This paragraph is long. So the sentences that comprise it are long.

(D) The members of the company are old. So the company itself is old.

(E) The atoms comprising this molecule are elements. So the molecule itself is an element.

GO ON TO THE NEXT PAGE.

8. A leading critic of space exploration contends that it would be wrong, given current technology, to send a group of explorers to Mars, since the explorers would be unlikely to survive the trip. But that exaggerates the risk. There would be a well-engineered backup system at every stage of the long and complicated journey. A fatal catastrophe is quite unlikely at any given stage if such a backup system is in place.

The reasoning in the argument is flawed in that the argument

(A) infers that something is true of a whole merely from the fact that it is true of each of the parts

(B) infers that something cannot occur merely from the fact that it is unlikely to occur

(C) draws a conclusion about what must be the case based on evidence about what is probably the case

(D) infers that something will work merely because it could work

(E) rejects a view merely on the grounds that an inadequate argument has been made for it

9. A retrospective study is a scientific study that tries to determine the causes of subjects' present characteristics by looking for significant connections between the present characteristics of subjects and what happened to those subjects in the past, before the study began. Because retrospective studies of human subjects must use the subjects' reports about their own pasts, however, such studies cannot reliably determine the causes of human subjects' present characteristics.

Which one of the following, if assumed, enables the argument's conclusion to be properly drawn?

(A) Whether or not a study of human subjects can reliably determine the causes of those subjects' present characteristics may depend at least in part on the extent to which that study uses inaccurate reports about the subjects' pasts.

(B) A retrospective study cannot reliably determine the causes of human subjects' present characteristics unless there exist correlations between the present characteristics of the subjects and what happened to those subjects in the past.

(C) In studies of human subjects that attempt to find connections between subjects' present characteristics and what happened to those subjects in the past, the subjects' reports about their own pasts are highly susceptible to inaccuracy.

(D) If a study of human subjects uses only accurate reports about the subjects' pasts, then that study can reliably determine the causes of those subjects' present characteristics.

(E) Every scientific study in which researchers look for significant connections between the present characteristics of subjects and what happened to those subjects in the past must use the subjects' reports about their own pasts.

GO ON TO THE NEXT PAGE.

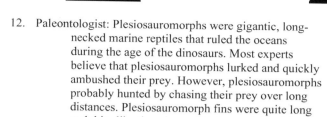

10. Gigantic passenger planes currently being developed will have enough space to hold shops and lounges in addition to passenger seating. However, the additional space will more likely be used for more passenger seating. The number of passengers flying the air-traffic system is expected to triple within 20 years, and it will be impossible for airports to accommodate enough normal-sized jet planes to carry that many passengers.

Which one of the following most accurately states the conclusion drawn in the argument?

(A) Gigantic planes currently being developed will have enough space in them to hold shops and lounges as well as passenger seating.

(B) The additional space in the gigantic planes currently being developed is more likely to be filled with passenger seating than with shops and lounges.

(C) The number of passengers flying the air-traffic system is expected to triple within 20 years.

(D) In 20 years, it will be impossible for airports to accommodate enough normal-sized planes to carry the number of passengers that are expected to be flying then.

(E) In 20 years, most airline passengers will be flying in gigantic passenger planes.

11. Scientist: To study the comparative effectiveness of two experimental medications for athlete's foot, a representative sample of people with athlete's foot were randomly assigned to one of two groups. One group received only medication M, and the other received only medication N. The only people whose athlete's foot was cured had been given medication M.

Reporter: This means, then, that if anyone in the study had athlete's foot that was not cured, that person did not receive medication M.

Which one of the following most accurately describes the reporter's error in reasoning?

(A) The reporter concludes from evidence showing only that M can cure athlete's foot that M always cures athlete's foot.

(B) The reporter illicitly draws a conclusion about the population as a whole on the basis of a study conducted only on a sample of the population.

(C) The reporter presumes, without providing justification, that medications M and N are available to people who have athlete's foot but did not participate in the study.

(D) The reporter fails to allow for the possibility that athlete's foot may be cured even if neither of the two medications studied is taken.

(E) The reporter presumes, without providing justification, that there is no sizeable subgroup of people whose athlete's foot will be cured only if they do not take medication M.

12. Paleontologist: Plesiosauromorphs were gigantic, long-necked marine reptiles that ruled the oceans during the age of the dinosaurs. Most experts believe that plesiosauromorphs lurked and quickly ambushed their prey. However, plesiosauromorphs probably hunted by chasing their prey over long distances. Plesiosauromorph fins were quite long and thin, like the wings of birds specialized for long-distance flight.

Which one of the following is an assumption on which the paleontologist's argument depends?

(A) Birds and reptiles share many physical features because they descend from common evolutionary ancestors.

(B) During the age of dinosaurs, plesiosauromorphs were the only marine reptiles that had long, thin fins.

(C) A gigantic marine animal would not be able to find enough food to meet the caloric requirements dictated by its body size if it did not hunt by chasing prey over long distances.

(D) Most marine animals that chase prey over long distances are specialized for long-distance swimming.

(E) The shape of a marine animal's fin affects the way the animal swims in the same way as the shape of a bird's wing affects the way the bird flies.

13. Buying elaborate screensavers—programs that put moving images on a computer monitor to prevent damage—can cost a company far more in employee time than it saves in electricity and monitor protection. Employees cannot resist spending time playing with screensavers that flash interesting graphics across their screens.

Which one of the following most closely conforms to the principle illustrated above?

(A) A school that chooses textbooks based on student preference may not get the most economical package.

(B) An energy-efficient insulation system may cost more up front but will ultimately save money over the life of the house.

(C) The time that it takes to have a pizza delivered may be longer than it takes to cook a complete dinner.

(D) A complicated hotel security system may cost more in customer goodwill than it saves in losses by theft.

(E) An electronic keyboard may be cheaper to buy than a piano but more expensive to repair.

GO ON TO THE NEXT PAGE.

14. Music professor: Because rap musicians can work alone in a recording studio, they need not accommodate supporting musicians' wishes. Further, learning to rap is not as formal a process as learning an instrument. Thus, rap is an extremely individualistic and nontraditional musical form.

    Music critic: But rap appeals to tradition by using bits of older songs. Besides, the themes and styles of rap have developed into a tradition. And successful rap musicians do not perform purely idiosyncratically but conform their work to the preferences of the public.

    The music critic's response to the music professor's argument

    (A)   challenges it by offering evidence against one of the stated premises on which its conclusion concerning rap music is based
    (B)   challenges its conclusion concerning rap music by offering certain additional observations that the music professor does not take into account in his argument
    (C)   challenges the grounds on which the music professor generalizes from the particular context of rap music to the broader context of musical tradition and individuality
    (D)   challenges it by offering an alternative explanation of phenomena that the music professor cites as evidence for his thesis about rap music
    (E)   challenges each of a group of claims about tradition and individuality in music that the music professor gives as evidence in his argument

15. Speaker: Like many contemporary critics, Smith argues that the true meaning of an author's statements can be understood only through insight into the author's social circumstances. But this same line of analysis can be applied to Smith's own words. Thus, if she is right we should be able, at least in part, to discern from Smith's social circumstances the "true meaning" of Smith's statements. This, in turn, suggests that Smith herself is not aware of the true meaning of her own words.

    The speaker's main conclusion logically follows if which one of the following is assumed?

    (A)   Insight into the intended meaning of an author's work is not as important as insight into its true meaning.
    (B)   Smith lacks insight into her own social circumstances.
    (C)   There is just one meaning that Smith intends her work to have.
    (D)   Smith's theory about the relation of social circumstances to the understanding of meaning lacks insight.
    (E)   The intended meaning of an author's work is not always good evidence of its true meaning.

16. Tissue biopsies taken on patients who have undergone throat surgery show that those who snored frequently were significantly more likely to have serious abnormalities in their throat muscles than those who snored rarely or not at all. This shows that snoring can damage the throat of the snorer.

    Which one of the following, if true, most strengthens the argument?

    (A)   The study relied on the subjects' self-reporting to determine whether or not they snored frequently.
    (B)   The patients' throat surgery was not undertaken to treat abnormalities in their throat muscles.
    (C)   All of the test subjects were of similar age and weight and in similar states of health.
    (D)   People who have undergone throat surgery are no more likely to snore than people who have not undergone throat surgery.
    (E)   The abnormalities in the throat muscles discovered in the study do not cause snoring.

GO ON TO THE NEXT PAGE.

17. One should never sacrifice one's health in order to acquire money, for without health, happiness is not obtainable.

The conclusion of the argument follows logically if which one of the following is assumed?

(A) Money should be acquired only if its acquisition will not make happiness unobtainable.

(B) In order to be happy one must have either money or health.

(C) Health should be valued only as a precondition for happiness.

(D) Being wealthy is, under certain conditions, conducive to unhappiness.

(E) Health is more conducive to happiness than wealth is.

18. Vanessa: All computer code must be written by a pair of programmers working at a single workstation. This is needed to prevent programmers from writing idiosyncratic code that can be understood only by the original programmer.

Jo: Most programming projects are kept afloat by the best programmers on the team, who are typically at least 100 times more productive than the worst. Since they generally work best when they work alone, the most productive programmers must be allowed to work by themselves.

Each of the following assignments of computer programmers is consistent both with the principle expressed by Vanessa and with the principle expressed by Jo EXCEPT:

(A) Olga and Kensuke are both programmers of roughly average productivity who feel that they are more productive when working alone. They have been assigned to work together at a single workstation.

(B) John is experienced but is not among the most productive programmers on the team. He has been assigned to mentor Tyrone, a new programmer who is not yet very productive. They are to work together at a single workstation.

(C) Although not among the most productive programmers on the team, Chris is more productive than Jennifer. They have been assigned to work together at a single workstation.

(D) Yolanda is the most productive programmer on the team. She has been assigned to work with Mike, who is also very productive. They are to work together at the same workstation.

(E) Kevin and Amy both have a reputation for writing idiosyncratic code; neither is unusually productive. They have been assigned to work together at the same workstation.

19. In West Calverton, most pet stores sell exotic birds, and most of those that sell exotic birds also sell tropical fish. However, any pet store there that sells tropical fish but not exotic birds does sell gerbils; and no independently owned pet stores in West Calverton sell gerbils.

If the statements above are true, which one of the following must be true?

(A) Most pet stores in West Calverton that are not independently owned do not sell exotic birds.

(B) No pet stores in West Calverton that sell tropical fish and exotic birds sell gerbils.

(C) Some pet stores in West Calverton that sell gerbils also sell exotic birds.

(D) No independently owned pet store in West Calverton sells tropical fish but not exotic birds.

(E) Any independently owned pet store in West Calverton that does not sell tropical fish sells exotic birds.

20. Astronomer: Earlier estimates of the distances of certain stars from Earth would mean that these stars are about 1 billion years older than the universe itself, an impossible scenario. My estimates of the distances indicate that these stars are much farther away than previously thought. And the farther away the stars are, the greater their intrinsic brightness must be, given their appearance to us on Earth. So the new estimates of these stars' distances from Earth help resolve the earlier conflict between the ages of these stars and the age of the universe.

Which one of the following, if true, most helps to explain why the astronomer's estimates of the stars' distances from Earth help resolve the earlier conflict between the ages of these stars and the age of the universe?

(A) The stars are the oldest objects yet discovered in the universe.

(B) The younger the universe is, the more bright stars it is likely to have.

(C) The brighter a star is, the younger it is.

(D) How bright celestial objects appear to be depends on how far away from the observer they are.

(E) New telescopes allow astronomers to see a greater number of distant stars.

GO ON TO THE NEXT PAGE.

21. Most large nurseries sell raspberry plants primarily to commercial raspberry growers and sell only plants that are guaranteed to be disease-free. However, the shipment of raspberry plants that Johnson received from Wally's Plants carried a virus that commonly afflicts raspberries.

Which one of the following is most strongly supported by the information above?

(A) If Johnson is a commercial raspberry grower and Wally's Plants is not a large nursery, then the shipment of raspberry plants that Johnson received was probably guaranteed to be disease-free.

(B) Johnson is probably not a commercial raspberry grower if the shipment of raspberry plants that Johnson received from Wally's Plants was not entirely as it was guaranteed to be.

(C) If Johnson is not a commercial raspberry grower, then Wally's Plants is probably not a large nursery.

(D) Wally's Plants is probably not a large, well-run nursery if it sells its raspberry plants primarily to commercial raspberry growers.

(E) If Wally's Plants is a large nursery, then the raspberry plants that Johnson received in the shipment were probably not entirely as they were guaranteed to be.

22. Drug company manager: Our newest product is just not selling. One way to save it would be a new marketing campaign. This would not guarantee success, but it is one chance to save the product, so we should try it.

Which one of the following, if true, most seriously weakens the manager's argument?

(A) The drug company has invested heavily in its newest product, and losses due to this product would be harmful to the company's profits.

(B) Many new products fail whether or not they are supported by marketing campaigns.

(C) The drug company should not undertake a new marketing campaign for its newest product if the campaign has no chance to succeed.

(D) Undertaking a new marketing campaign would endanger the drug company's overall position by necessitating cutbacks in existing marketing campaigns.

(E) Consumer demand for the drug company's other products has been strong in the time since the company's newest product was introduced.

23. Consumer advocate: TMD, a pesticide used on peaches, shows no effects on human health when it is ingested in the amount present in the per capita peach consumption in this country. But while 80 percent of the population eat no peaches, others, including small children, consume much more than the national average, and thus ingest disproportionately large amounts of TMD. So even though the use of TMD on peaches poses minimal risk to most of the population, it has not been shown to be an acceptable practice.

Which one of the following principles, if valid, most helps to justify the consumer advocate's argumentation?

(A) The possibility that more data about a pesticide's health effects might reveal previously unknown risks at low doses warrants caution in assessing that pesticide's overall risks.

(B) The consequences of using a pesticide are unlikely to be acceptable when a majority of the population is likely to ingest it.

(C) Use of a pesticide is acceptable only if it is used for its intended purpose and the pesticide has been shown not to harm any portion of the population.

(D) Society has a special obligation to protect small children from pesticides unless average doses received by the population are low and have not been shown to be harmful to children's health.

(E) Measures taken to protect the population from a harm sometimes turn out to be the cause of a more serious harm to certain segments of the population.

24. Legal commentator: The goal of a recently enacted law that bans smoking in workplaces is to protect employees from secondhand smoke. But the law is written in such a way that it cannot be interpreted as ever prohibiting people from smoking in their own homes.

The statements above, if true, provide a basis for rejecting which one of the following claims?

(A) The law will be interpreted in a way that is inconsistent with the intentions of the legislators who supported it.

(B) Supporters of the law believe that it will have a significant impact on the health of many workers.

(C) The law offers no protection from secondhand smoke for people outside of their workplaces.

(D) Most people believe that smokers have a fundamental right to smoke in their own homes.

(E) The law will protect domestic workers such as housecleaners from secondhand smoke in their workplaces.

GO ON TO THE NEXT PAGE.

25. University president: Our pool of applicants has been shrinking over the past few years. One possible explanation of this unwelcome phenomenon is that we charge too little for tuition and fees. Prospective students and their parents conclude that the quality of education they would receive at this institution is not as high as that offered by institutions with higher tuition. So, if we want to increase the size of our applicant pool, we need to raise our tuition and fees.

The university president's argument requires the assumption that

(A)   the proposed explanation for the decline in applications applies in this case
(B)   the quality of a university education is dependent on the amount of tuition charged by the university
(C)   an increase in tuition and fees at the university would guarantee a larger applicant pool
(D)   there is no additional explanation for the university's shrinking applicant pool
(E)   the amount charged by the university for tuition has not increased in recent years

26. Editorial: It has been suggested that private, for-profit companies should be hired to supply clean drinking water to areas of the world where it is unavailable now. But water should not be supplied by private companies. After all, clean water is essential for human health, and the purpose of a private company is to produce profit, not to promote health.

Which one of the following principles, if valid, would most help to justify the reasoning in the editorial?

(A)   A private company should not be allowed to supply a commodity that is essential to human health unless that commodity is also supplied by a government agency.
(B)   If something is essential for human health and private companies are unwilling or unable to supply it, then it should be supplied by a government agency.
(C)   Drinking water should never be supplied by an organization that is not able to consistently supply clean, safe water.
(D)   The mere fact that something actually promotes human health is not sufficient to show that its purpose is to promote health.
(E)   If something is necessary for human health, then it should be provided by an organization whose primary purpose is the promotion of health.

S T O P
IF YOU FINISH BEFORE TIME IS CALLED, YOU MAY CHECK YOUR WORK ON THIS SECTION ONLY.
DO NOT WORK ON ANY OTHER SECTION IN THE TEST.

SECTION III
Time—35 minutes
23 Questions

Directions: Each group of questions in this section is based on a set of conditions. In answering some of the questions, it may be useful to draw a rough diagram. Choose the response that most accurately and completely answers each question and blacken the corresponding space on your answer sheet.

Questions 1–6

A motel operator is scheduling appointments to start up services at a new motel. Appointments for six services—gas, landscaping, power, satellite, telephone, and water—will be scheduled, one appointment per day for the next six days. The schedule for the appointments is subject to the following conditions:

The water appointment must be scheduled for an earlier day than the landscaping appointment.

The power appointment must be scheduled for an earlier day than both the gas and satellite appointments.

The appointments scheduled for the second and third days cannot be for either gas, satellite, or telephone.

The telephone appointment cannot be scheduled for the sixth day.

1. Which one of the following is an acceptable schedule of appointments, listed in order from earliest to latest?

   (A) gas, water, power, telephone, landscaping, satellite
   (B) power, water, landscaping, gas, satellite, telephone
   (C) telephone, power, landscaping, gas, water, satellite
   (D) telephone, water, power, landscaping, gas, satellite
   (E) water, telephone, power, gas, satellite, landscaping

2. If neither the gas nor the satellite nor the telephone appointment is scheduled for the fourth day, which one of the following must be true?

   (A) The gas appointment is scheduled for the fifth day.
   (B) The power appointment is scheduled for the third day.
   (C) The satellite appointment is scheduled for the sixth day.
   (D) The telephone appointment is scheduled for the first day.
   (E) The water appointment is scheduled for the second day.

3. Which one of the following must be true?

   (A) The landscaping appointment is scheduled for an earlier day than the telephone appointment.
   (B) The power appointment is scheduled for an earlier day than the landscaping appointment.
   (C) The telephone appointment is scheduled for an earlier day than the gas appointment.
   (D) The telephone appointment is scheduled for an earlier day than the water appointment.
   (E) The water appointment is scheduled for an earlier day than the gas appointment.

4. Which one of the following CANNOT be the appointments scheduled for the fourth, fifth, and sixth days, listed in that order?

   (A) gas, satellite, landscaping
   (B) landscaping, satellite, gas
   (C) power, satellite, gas
   (D) telephone, satellite, gas
   (E) water, gas, landscaping

5. If neither the gas appointment nor the satellite appointment is scheduled for the sixth day, which one of the following must be true?

   (A) The gas appointment is scheduled for the fifth day.
   (B) The landscaping appointment is scheduled for the sixth day.
   (C) The power appointment is scheduled for the third day.
   (D) The telephone appointment is scheduled for the fourth day.
   (E) The water appointment is scheduled for the second day.

6. Which one of the following, if substituted for the condition that the telephone appointment cannot be scheduled for the sixth day, would have the same effect in determining the order of the appointments?

   (A) The telephone appointment must be scheduled for an earlier day than the gas appointment or the satellite appointment, or both.
   (B) The telephone appointment must be scheduled for the day immediately before either the gas appointment or the satellite appointment.
   (C) The telephone appointment must be scheduled for an earlier day than the landscaping appointment.
   (D) If the telephone appointment is not scheduled for the first day, it must be scheduled for the day immediately before the gas appointment.
   (E) Either the gas appointment or the satellite appointment must be scheduled for the sixth day.

GO ON TO THE NEXT PAGE.

Questions 7–13

An artisan has been hired to create three stained glass windows. The artisan will use exactly five colors of glass: green, orange, purple, rose, and yellow. Each color of glass will be used at least once, and each window will contain at least two different colors of glass. The windows must also conform to the following conditions:

Exactly one of the windows contains both green glass and purple glass.

Exactly two of the windows contain rose glass.

If a window contains yellow glass, then that window contains neither green glass nor orange glass.

If a window does not contain purple glass, then that window contains orange glass.

7. Which one of the following could be the color combinations of the glass in the three windows?

(A) window 1: green, purple, rose, and orange
window 2: rose and yellow
window 3: green and orange

(B) window 1: green, purple, and rose
window 2: green, rose, and orange
window 3: purple and yellow

(C) window 1: green, purple, and rose
window 2: green, purple, and orange
window 3: purple, rose, and yellow

(D) window 1: green, purple, and orange
window 2: rose, orange, and yellow
window 3: purple and rose

(E) window 1: green, purple, and orange
window 2: purple, rose, and yellow
window 3: purple and orange

8. Which one of the following CANNOT be the complete color combination of the glass in one of the windows?

(A) green and orange
(B) green and purple
(C) green and rose
(D) purple and orange
(E) rose and orange

9. If two of the windows are made with exactly two colors of glass each, then the complete color combination of the glass in one of those windows could be

(A) rose and yellow
(B) orange and rose
(C) orange and purple
(D) green and rose
(E) green and orange

10. If the complete color combination of the glass in one of the windows is purple, rose, and orange, then the complete color combination of the glass in one of the other windows could be

(A) green, orange, and rose
(B) green, orange, and purple
(C) orange and rose
(D) orange and purple
(E) green and orange

11. If orange glass is used in more of the windows than green glass, then the complete color combination of the glass in one of the windows could be

(A) orange and purple
(B) green, purple, and rose
(C) green and purple
(D) green and orange
(E) green, orange, and rose

12. Which one of the following could be used in all three windows?

(A) green glass
(B) orange glass
(C) purple glass
(D) rose glass
(E) yellow glass

13. If none of the windows contains both rose glass and orange glass, then the complete color combination of the glass in one of the windows must be

(A) green and purple
(B) green, purple, and orange
(C) green and orange
(D) purple and orange
(E) purple, rose, and yellow

GO ON TO THE NEXT PAGE.

Questions 14–18

A conference on management skills consists of exactly five talks, which are held successively in the following order: Feedback, Goal Sharing, Handling People, Information Overload, and Leadership. Exactly four employees of SoftCorp—Quigley, Rivera, Spivey, and Tran—each attend exactly two of the talks. No talk is attended by more than two of the employees, who attend the talks in accordance with the following conditions:

Quigley attends neither Feedback nor Handling People.
Rivera attends neither Goal Sharing nor Handling People.
Spivey does not attend either of the talks that Tran attends.
Quigley attends the first talk Tran attends.
Spivey attends the first talk Rivera attends.

14. Which one of the following could be a complete and accurate matching of the talks to the SoftCorp employees who attend them?

(A) Feedback: Rivera, Spivey
Goal Sharing: Quigley, Tran
Handling People: None
Information Overload: Quigley, Rivera
Leadership: Spivey, Tran
(B) Feedback: Rivera, Spivey
Goal Sharing: Quigley, Tran
Handling People: Rivera, Tran
Information Overload: Quigley
Leadership: Spivey
(C) Feedback: Rivera, Spivey
Goal Sharing: Quigley, Tran
Handling People: Tran
Information Overload: Quigley, Rivera
Leadership: Spivey
(D) Feedback: Rivera, Spivey
Goal Sharing: Tran
Handling People: Tran
Information Overload: Quigley, Rivera
Leadership: Quigley, Spivey
(E) Feedback: Spivey
Goal Sharing: Quigley, Tran
Handling People: Spivey
Information Overload: Quigley, Rivera
Leadership: Rivera, Tran

15. If none of the SoftCorp employees attends Handling People, then which one of the following must be true?

(A) Rivera attends Feedback.
(B) Rivera attends Leadership.
(C) Spivey attends Information Overload.
(D) Tran attends Goal Sharing.
(E) Tran attends Information Overload.

16. Which one of the following is a complete and accurate list of the talks any one of which Rivera and Spivey could attend together?

(A) Feedback, Information Overload, Leadership
(B) Feedback, Goal Sharing, Information Overload
(C) Information Overload, Leadership
(D) Feedback, Leadership
(E) Feedback, Information Overload

17. If Quigley is the only SoftCorp employee to attend Leadership, then which one of the following could be false?

(A) Rivera attends Feedback.
(B) Rivera attends Information Overload.
(C) Spivey attends Feedback.
(D) Spivey attends Handling People.
(E) Tran attends Goal Sharing.

18. If Rivera is the only SoftCorp employee to attend Information Overload, then which one of the following could be false?

(A) Quigley attends Leadership.
(B) Rivera attends Feedback.
(C) Spivey attends Feedback.
(D) Tran attends Goal Sharing.
(E) Tran attends Handling People.

GO ON TO THE NEXT PAGE.

Questions 19–23

Exactly six witnesses will testify in a trial: Mangione, Ramirez, Sanderson, Tannenbaum, Ujemori, and Wong. The witnesses will testify one by one, and each only once. The order in which the witnesses testify is subject to the following constraints:

Sanderson must testify immediately before either Tannenbaum or Ujemori.

Ujemori must testify earlier than both Ramirez and Wong.

Either Tannenbaum or Wong must testify immediately before Mangione.

19. Which one of the following lists the witnesses in an order in which they could testify?

(A) Ramirez, Sanderson, Tannenbaum, Mangione, Ujemori, Wong
(B) Sanderson, Tannenbaum, Ujemori, Ramirez, Wong, Mangione
(C) Sanderson, Ujemori, Tannenbaum, Wong, Ramirez, Mangione
(D) Tannenbaum, Mangione, Ujemori, Sanderson, Ramirez, Wong
(E) Wong, Ramirez, Sanderson, Tannenbaum, Mangione, Ujemori

20. If Tannenbaum testifies first, then which one of the following could be true?

(A) Ramirez testifies second.
(B) Wong testifies third.
(C) Sanderson testifies fourth.
(D) Ujemori testifies fifth.
(E) Mangione testifies sixth.

21. If Sanderson testifies fifth, then Ujemori must testify

(A) first
(B) second
(C) third
(D) fourth
(E) sixth

22. Which one of the following pairs of witnesses CANNOT testify third and fourth, respectively?

(A) Mangione, Tannenbaum
(B) Ramirez, Sanderson
(C) Sanderson, Ujemori
(D) Tannenbaum, Ramirez
(E) Ujemori, Wong

23. Which one of the following pairs of witnesses CANNOT testify first and second, respectively?

(A) Sanderson, Ujemori
(B) Tannenbaum, Mangione
(C) Tannenbaum, Sanderson
(D) Ujemori, Tannenbaum
(E) Ujemori, Wong

STOP
IF YOU FINISH BEFORE TIME IS CALLED, YOU MAY CHECK YOUR WORK ON THIS SECTION ONLY.
DO NOT WORK ON ANY OTHER SECTION IN THE TEST.

SECTION IV

Time—35 minutes

26 Questions

<u>Directions:</u> The questions in this section are based on the reasoning contained in brief statements or passages. For some questions, more than one of the choices could conceivably answer the question. However, you are to choose the <u>best</u> answer; that is, the response that most accurately and completely answers the question. You should not make assumptions that are by commonsense standards implausible, superfluous, or incompatible with the passage. After you have chosen the best answer, blacken the corresponding space on your answer sheet.

1. Marine biologist: Scientists have long wondered why the fish that live around coral reefs exhibit such brilliant colors. One suggestion is that coral reefs are colorful and, therefore, that colorful fish are camouflaged by them. Many animal species, after all, use camouflage to avoid predators. However, as regards the populations around reefs, this suggestion is mistaken. A reef stripped of its fish is quite monochromatic. Most corals, it turns out, are relatively dull browns and greens.

    Which one of the following most accurately expresses the main conclusion drawn in the marine biologist's argument?

    (A)   One hypothesis about why fish living near coral reefs exhibit such bright colors is that the fish are camouflaged by their bright colors.
    (B)   The fact that many species use camouflage to avoid predators is one reason to believe that brightly colored fish living near reefs do too.
    (C)   The suggestion that the fish living around coral reefs exhibit bright colors because they are camouflaged by the reefs is mistaken.
    (D)   A reef stripped of its fish is relatively monochromatic.
    (E)   It turns out that the corals in a coral reef are mostly dull hues of brown and green.

2. To discover what percentage of teenagers believe in telekinesis—the psychic ability to move objects without physically touching them—a recent survey asked a representative sample of teenagers whether they agreed with the following statement: "A person's thoughts can influence the movement of physical objects." But because this statement is particularly ambiguous and is amenable to a naturalistic, uncontroversial interpretation, the survey's responses are also ambiguous.

    The reasoning above conforms most closely to which one of the following general propositions?

    (A)   Uncontroversial statements are useless in surveys.
    (B)   Every statement is amenable to several interpretations.
    (C)   Responses to surveys are always unambiguous if the survey's questions are well phrased.
    (D)   Responses people give to poorly phrased questions are likely to be ambiguous.
    (E)   Statements about psychic phenomena can always be given naturalistic interpretations.

GO ON TO THE NEXT PAGE.

3. A recent study of perfect pitch—the ability to identify the pitch of an isolated musical note—found that a high percentage of people who have perfect pitch are related to someone else who has it. Among those without perfect pitch, the percentage was much lower. This shows that having perfect pitch is a consequence of genetic factors.

Which one of the following, if true, most strengthens the argument?

(A) People who have relatives with perfect pitch generally receive no more musical training than do others.

(B) All of the researchers conducting the study had perfect pitch.

(C) People with perfect pitch are more likely than others to choose music as a career.

(D) People with perfect pitch are more likely than others to make sure that their children receive musical training.

(E) People who have some training in music are more likely to have perfect pitch than those with no such training.

4. Paleontologists recently excavated two corresponding sets of dinosaur tracks, one left by a large grazing dinosaur and the other by a smaller predatory dinosaur. The two sets of tracks make abrupt turns repeatedly in tandem, suggesting that the predator was following the grazing dinosaur and had matched its stride. Modern predatory mammals, such as lions, usually match the stride of prey they are chasing immediately before they strike those prey. This suggests that the predatory dinosaur was chasing the grazing dinosaur and attacked immediately afterwards.

Which one of the following most accurately describes the role played in the argument by the statement that the predatory dinosaur was following the grazing dinosaur and had matched its stride?

(A) It helps establish the scientific importance of the argument's overall conclusion, but is not offered as evidence for that conclusion.

(B) It is a hypothesis that is rejected in favor of the hypothesis stated in the argument's overall conclusion.

(C) It provides the basis for an analogy used in support of the argument's overall conclusion.

(D) It is presented to counteract a possible objection to the argument's overall conclusion.

(E) It is the overall conclusion of the argument.

5. Researchers announced recently that over the past 25 years the incidence of skin cancer caused by exposure to harmful rays from the sun has continued to grow in spite of the increasingly widespread use of sunscreens. This shows that using sunscreen is unlikely to reduce a person's risk of developing such skin cancer.

Which one of the following, if true, most weakens the argument?

(A) Most people who purchase a sunscreen product will not purchase the most expensive brand available.

(B) Skin cancer generally develops among the very old as a result of sunburns experienced when very young.

(C) The development of sunscreens by pharmaceutical companies was based upon research conducted by dermatologists.

(D) People who know that they are especially susceptible to skin cancer are generally disinclined to spend a large amount of time in the sun.

(E) Those who use sunscreens most regularly are people who believe themselves to be most susceptible to skin cancer.

6. University administrator: Any proposal for a new department will not be funded if there are fewer than 50 people per year available for hire in that field and the proposed department would duplicate more than 25 percent of the material covered in one of our existing departments. The proposed Area Studies Department will duplicate more than 25 percent of the material covered in our existing Anthropology Department. However, we will fund the new department.

Which one of the following statements follows logically from the university administrator's statements?

(A) The field of Area Studies has at least 50 people per year available for hire.

(B) The proposed Area Studies Department would not duplicate more than 25 percent of the material covered in any existing department other than Anthropology.

(C) If the proposed Area Studies Department did not duplicate more than 25 percent of the material covered in Anthropology, then the new department would not be funded.

(D) The Anthropology Department duplicates more than 25 percent of the material covered in the proposed Area Studies Department.

(E) The field of Area Studies has fewer than 50 people per year available for hire.

GO ON TO THE NEXT PAGE.

7. Researcher: Over the course of three decades, we kept records of the average beak size of two populations of the same species of bird, one wild population, the other captive. During this period, the average beak size of the captive birds did not change, while the average beak size of the wild birds decreased significantly.

Which one of the following, if true, most helps to explain the researcher's findings?

(A) The small-beaked wild birds were easier to capture and measure than the large-beaked wild birds.

(B) The large-beaked wild birds were easier to capture and measure than the small-beaked wild birds.

(C) Changes in the wild birds' food supply during the study period favored the survival of small-beaked birds over large-beaked birds.

(D) The average body size of the captive birds remained the same over the study period.

(E) The researcher measured the beaks of some of the wild birds on more than one occasion.

8. Storytelling appears to be a universal aspect of both past and present cultures. Comparative study of traditional narratives from widely separated epochs and diverse cultures reveals common themes such as creation, tribal origin, mystical beings and quasi-historical figures, and common story types such as fables and tales in which animals assume human personalities.

The evidence cited above from the study of traditional narratives most supports which one of the following statements?

(A) Storytellers routinely borrow themes from other cultures.

(B) Storytellers have long understood that the narrative is a universal aspect of human culture.

(C) Certain human concerns and interests arise in all of the world's cultures.

(D) Storytelling was no less important in ancient cultures than it is in modern cultures.

(E) The best way to understand a culture is to understand what motivates its storytellers.

9. If a mother's first child is born before its due date, it is likely that her second child will be also. Jackie's second child was not born before its due date, so it is likely that Jackie's first child was not born before its due date either.

The questionable reasoning in the argument above is most similar in its reasoning to which one of the following?

(A) Artisans who finish their projects before the craft fair will probably go to the craft fair. Ben will not finish his project before the fair. So he probably will not go to the craft fair.

(B) All responsible pet owners are likely to be good with children. So anyone who is good with children is probably a responsible pet owner.

(C) If a movie is a box-office hit, it is likely that its sequel will be also. *Hawkman II*, the sequel to *Hawkman I*, was not a box-office hit, so *Hawkman I* was probably not a box-office hit.

(D) If a business is likely to fail, people will not invest in it. Pallid Starr is likely to fail, therefore no one is likely to invest in it.

(E) Tai will go sailing only if the weather is nice. The weather will be nice, thus Tai will probably go sailing.

10. Science journalist: Europa, a moon of Jupiter, is covered with ice. Data recently transmitted by a spacecraft strongly suggest that there are oceans of liquid water deep under the ice. Life as we know it could evolve only in the presence of liquid water. Hence, it is likely that at least primitive life has evolved on Europa.

The science journalist's argument is most vulnerable to criticism on the grounds that it

(A) takes for granted that if a condition would be necessary for the evolution of life as we know it, then such life could not have evolved anywhere that this condition does not hold

(B) fails to address adequately the possibility that there are conditions necessary for the evolution of life in addition to the presence of liquid water

(C) takes for granted that life is likely to be present on Europa if, but only if, life evolved on Europa

(D) overlooks the possibility that there could be unfamiliar forms of life that have evolved without the presence of liquid water

(E) takes for granted that no conditions on Europa other than the supposed presence of liquid water could have accounted for the data transmitted by the spacecraft

GO ON TO THE NEXT PAGE.

4 4 4 4 4 -65- 4

11. A bacterial species will inevitably develop greater resistance within a few years to any antibiotics used against it, unless those antibiotics eliminate that species completely. However, no single antibiotic now on the market is powerful enough to eliminate bacterial species X completely.

Which one of the following is most strongly supported by the statements above?

(A) It is unlikely that any antibiotic can be developed that will completely eliminate bacterial species X.

(B) If any antibiotic now on the market is used against bacterial species X, that species will develop greater resistance to it within a few years.

(C) The only way of completely eliminating bacterial species X is by a combination of two or more antibiotics now on the market.

(D) Bacterial species X will inevitably become more virulent in the course of time.

(E) Bacterial species X is more resistant to at least some antibiotics that have been used against it than it was before those antibiotics were used against it.

12. Political scientist: It is not uncommon for a politician to criticize his or her political opponents by claiming that their exposition of their ideas is muddled and incomprehensible. Such criticism, however, is never sincere. Political agendas promoted in a manner that cannot be understood by large numbers of people will not be realized for, as every politician knows, political mobilization requires commonality of purpose.

Which one of the following is the most accurate rendering of the political scientist's main conclusion?

(A) People who promote political agendas in an incomprehensible manner should be regarded as insincere.

(B) Sincere critics of the proponents of a political agenda should not focus their criticisms on the manner in which that agenda is promoted.

(C) The ineffectiveness of a confusingly promoted political agenda is a reason for refraining from, rather than engaging in, criticism of those who are promoting it.

(D) A politician criticizing his or her political opponents for presenting their political agendas in an incomprehensible manner is being insincere.

(E) To mobilize large numbers of people in support of a political agenda, that political agenda must be presented in such a way that it cannot be misunderstood.

13. Many symptoms of mental illnesses are affected by organic factors such as a deficiency in a compound in the brain. What is surprising, however, is the tremendous variation among different countries in the incidence of these symptoms in people with mental illnesses. This variation establishes that the organic factors that affect symptoms of mental illnesses are not distributed evenly around the globe.

The reasoning above is most vulnerable to criticism on the grounds that it

(A) does not say how many different mental illnesses are being discussed

(B) neglects the possibility that nutritional factors that contribute to deficiencies in compounds in the brain vary from culture to culture

(C) fails to consider the possibility that cultural factors significantly affect how mental illnesses manifest themselves in symptoms

(D) presumes, without providing justification, that any change in brain chemistry manifests itself as a change in mental condition

(E) presumes, without providing justification, that mental phenomena are only manifestations of physical phenomena

14. Politician: It has been proposed that the national parks in our country be managed by private companies rather than the government. A similar privatization of the telecommunications industry has benefited consumers by allowing competition among a variety of telephone companies to improve service and force down prices. Therefore, the privatization of the national parks would probably benefit park visitors as well.

Which one of the following, if true, most weakens the politician's argument?

(A) It would not be politically expedient to privatize the national parks even if doing so would, in the long run, improve service and reduce the fees charged to visitors.

(B) The privatization of the telecommunications industry has been problematic in that it has led to significantly increased unemployment and economic instability in that industry.

(C) The vast majority of people visiting the national parks are unaware of proposals to privatize the management of those parks.

(D) Privatizing the national parks would benefit a much smaller number of consumers to a much smaller extent than did the privatization of the telecommunications industry.

(E) The privatization of the national parks would produce much less competition between different companies than did the privatization of the telecommunications industry.

GO ON TO THE NEXT PAGE.

15. Jewel collectors, fearing that their eyes will be deceived by a counterfeit, will not buy a diamond unless the dealer guarantees that it is genuine. But why should a counterfeit give any less aesthetic pleasure when the naked eye cannot distinguish it from a real diamond? Both jewels should be deemed of equal value.

Which one of the following principles, if valid, most helps to justify the reasoning in the argument above?

(A) Jewel collectors should collect only those jewels that provide the most aesthetic pleasure.

(B) The value of a jewel should depend at least partly on market demand.

(C) It should not be assumed that everyone who likes diamonds receives the same degree of aesthetic pleasure from them.

(D) The value of a jewel should derive solely from the aesthetic pleasure it provides.

(E) Jewel collectors should not buy counterfeit jewels unless they are unable to distinguish counterfeit jewels from real ones.

16. All etching tools are either pin-tipped or bladed. While some bladed etching tools are used for engraving, some are not. On the other hand, all pin-tipped etching tools are used for engraving. Thus, there are more etching tools that are used for engraving than there are etching tools that are not used for engraving.

The conclusion of the argument follows logically if which one of the following is assumed?

(A) All tools used for engraving are etching tools as well.

(B) There are as many pin-tipped etching tools as there are bladed etching tools.

(C) No etching tool is both pin-tipped and bladed.

(D) The majority of bladed etching tools are not used for engraving.

(E) All etching tools that are not used for engraving are bladed.

17. A 24-year study of 1,500 adults showed that those subjects with a high intake of foods rich in beta-carotene were much less likely to die from cancer or heart disease than were those with a low intake of such foods. On the other hand, taking beta-carotene supplements for 12 years had no positive or negative effect on the health of subjects in a separate study of 20,000 adults.

Each of the following, if true, would help to resolve the apparent discrepancy between the results of the two studies EXCEPT:

(A) The human body processes the beta-carotene present in foods much more efficiently than it does beta-carotene supplements.

(B) Beta-carotene must be taken for longer than 12 years to have any cancer-preventive effects.

(C) Foods rich in beta-carotene also tend to contain other nutrients that assist in the human body's absorption of beta-carotene.

(D) In the 12-year study, half of the subjects were given beta-carotene supplements and half were given a placebo.

(E) In the 24-year study, the percentage of the subjects who had a high intake of beta-carotene-rich foods who smoked cigarettes was much smaller than the percentage of the subjects with a low intake of beta-carotene-rich foods who smoked.

GO ON TO THE NEXT PAGE.

18. If there are sentient beings on planets outside our solar system, we will not be able to determine this anytime in the near future unless some of these beings are at least as intelligent as humans. We will not be able to send spacecraft to planets outside our solar system anytime in the near future, and any sentient being on another planet capable of communicating with us anytime in the near future would have to be at least as intelligent as we are.

The argument's conclusion can be properly inferred if which one of the following is assumed?

(A) There are no sentient beings on planets in our solar system other than those on Earth.

(B) Any beings that are at least as intelligent as humans would want to communicate with sentient beings outside their own solar systems.

(C) If there is a sentient being on another planet that is as intelligent as humans are, we will not be able to send spacecraft to the being's planet anytime in the near future.

(D) If a sentient being on another planet cannot communicate with us, then the only way to detect its existence is by sending a spacecraft to its planet.

(E) Any sentient beings on planets outside our solar system that are at least as intelligent as humans would be capable of communicating with us.

19. Doctor: Medical researchers recently examined a large group of individuals who said that they had never experienced serious back pain. Half of the members of the group turned out to have bulging or slipped disks in their spines, conditions often blamed for serious back pain. Since these individuals with bulging or slipped disks evidently felt no pain from them, these conditions could not lead to serious back pain in people who do experience such pain.

The reasoning in the doctor's argument is most vulnerable to the criticism that it fails to consider which one of the following possibilities?

(A) A factor that need not be present in order for a certain effect to arise may nonetheless be sufficient to produce that effect.

(B) A factor that is not in itself sufficient to produce a certain effect may nonetheless be partly responsible for that effect in some instances.

(C) An effect that occurs in the absence of a particular phenomenon might not occur when that phenomenon is present.

(D) A characteristic found in half of a given sample of the population might not occur in half of the entire population.

(E) A factor that does not bring about a certain effect may nonetheless be more likely to be present when the effect occurs than when the effect does not occur.

20. Many workers who handled substance T in factories became seriously ill years later. We now know T caused at least some of their illnesses. Earlier ignorance of this connection does not absolve T's manufacturer of all responsibility. For had it investigated the safety of T before allowing workers to be exposed to it, many of their illnesses would have been prevented.

Which one of the following principles most helps to justify the conclusion above?

(A) Employees who are harmed by substances they handle on the job should be compensated for medical costs they incur as a result.

(B) Manufacturers should be held responsible only for the preventable consequences of their actions.

(C) Manufacturers have an obligation to inform workers of health risks of which they are aware.

(D) Whether or not an action's consequences were preventable is irrelevant to whether a manufacturer should be held responsible for those consequences.

(E) Manufacturers should be held responsible for the consequences of any of their actions that harm innocent people if those consequences were preventable.

21. It is virtually certain that the government contract for building the new highway will be awarded to either Phoenix Contracting or Cartwright Company. I have just learned that the government has decided not to award the contract to Cartwright Company. It is therefore almost inevitable that Phoenix Contracting will be awarded the contract.

The argument proceeds by

(A) concluding that it is extremely likely that an event will occur by ruling out the only probable alternative

(B) inferring, from a claim that one of two possible events will occur, that the other event will not occur

(C) refuting a claim that a particular event is inevitable by establishing the possibility of an alternative event

(D) predicting a future event on the basis of an established pattern of past events

(E) inferring a claim about the probability of a particular event from a general statistical statement

GO ON TO THE NEXT PAGE.

22. Researchers have found that children in large families—particularly the younger siblings—generally have fewer allergies than children in small families do. They hypothesize that exposure to germs during infancy makes people less likely to develop allergies.

Which one of the following, if true, most supports the researchers' hypothesis?

(A) In countries where the average number of children per family has decreased over the last century, the incidence of allergies has increased.

(B) Children in small families generally eat more kinds of very allergenic foods than children in large families do.

(C) Some allergies are life threatening, while many diseases caused by germs produce only temporary discomfort.

(D) Children whose parents have allergies have an above-average likelihood of developing allergies themselves.

(E) Children from small families who entered day care before age one were less likely to develop allergies than children from small families who entered day care later.

23. Film preservation requires transferring old movies from their original material—unstable, deteriorating nitrate film—to stable acetate film. But this is a time-consuming, expensive process, and there is no way to transfer all currently deteriorating nitrate films to acetate before they disintegrate. So some films from the earliest years of Hollywood will not be preserved.

Which one of the following is an assumption on which the argument depends?

(A) No new technology for transferring old movies from nitrate film to acetate film will ever be developed.

(B) Transferring films from nitrate to acetate is not the least expensive way of preserving them.

(C) Not many films from the earliest years of Hollywood have already been transferred to acetate.

(D) Some films from the earliest years of Hollywood currently exist solely in their original material.

(E) The least popular films from the earliest years of Hollywood are the ones most likely to be lost.

24. In a recent study of arthritis, researchers tried but failed to find any correlation between pain intensity and any of those features of the weather—humidity, temperature swings, barometric pressure—usually cited by arthritis sufferers as the cause of their increased pain. Those arthritis sufferers in the study who were convinced of the existence of such a correlation gave widely varying accounts of the time delay between the occurrence of what they believed to be the relevant feature of the weather and the increased intensity of the pain. Thus, this study _____.

Of the following, which one most logically completes the argument?

(A) indicates that the weather affects some arthritis sufferers more quickly than it does other arthritis sufferers

(B) indicates that arthritis sufferers' beliefs about the causes of the pain they feel may affect their assessment of the intensity of that pain

(C) suggests that arthritis sufferers are imagining the correlation they assert to exist

(D) suggests that some people are more susceptible to weather-induced arthritis pain than are others

(E) suggests that the scientific investigation of possible links between weather and arthritis pain is impossible

GO ON TO THE NEXT PAGE.

25. Cities with healthy economies typically have plenty of job openings. Cities with high-technology businesses also tend to have healthy economies, so those in search of jobs should move to a city with high-technology businesses.

The reasoning in which one of the following is most similar to the reasoning in the argument above?

(A)   Older antiques are usually the most valuable. Antique dealers generally authenticate the age of the antiques they sell, so those collectors who want the most valuable antiques should purchase their antiques from antique dealers.

(B)   Antique dealers who authenticate the age of the antiques they sell typically have plenty of antiques for sale. Since the most valuable antiques are those that have had their ages authenticated, antique collectors in search of valuable antiques should purchase their antiques from antique dealers.

(C)   Antiques that have had their ages authenticated tend to be valuable. Since antique dealers generally carry antiques that have had their ages authenticated, those collectors who want antiques that are valuable should purchase their antiques from antique dealers.

(D)   Many antique collectors know that antique dealers can authenticate the age of the antiques they sell. Since antiques that have had their ages authenticated are always the most valuable, most antique collectors who want antiques that are valuable tend to purchase their antiques from antique dealers.

(E)   Many antiques increase in value once they have had their ages authenticated by antique dealers. Since antique dealers tend to have plenty of valuable antiques, antique collectors who prefer to purchase the most valuable antiques should purchase antiques from antique dealers.

26. Sociologist: A recent study of 5,000 individuals found, on the basis of a physical exam, that more than 25 percent of people older than 65 were malnourished, though only 12 percent of the people in this age group fell below government poverty standards. In contrast, a greater percentage of the people 65 or younger fell below poverty standards than were found in the study to be malnourished.

Each of the following, if true, helps to explain the findings of the study cited by the sociologist EXCEPT:

(A)   Doctors are less likely to correctly diagnose and treat malnutrition in their patients who are over 65 than in their younger patients.

(B)   People over 65 are more likely to take medications that increase their need for certain nutrients than are people 65 or younger.

(C)   People over 65 are more likely to suffer from loss of appetite due to medication than are people 65 or younger.

(D)   People 65 or younger are no more likely to fall below government poverty standards than are people over 65.

(E)   People 65 or younger are less likely to have medical conditions that interfere with their digestion than are people over 65.

S T O P
IF YOU FINISH BEFORE TIME IS CALLED, YOU MAY CHECK YOUR WORK ON THIS SECTION ONLY.
DO NOT WORK ON ANY OTHER SECTION IN THE TEST.

ACKNOWLEDGMENTS

Acknowledgment is made to the following sources from which material has been adapted for use in this test booklet:

Richard H. Brodhead, *Cultures of Letters: Scenes of Reading and Writing in Nineteenth-Century America.* ©1993 by the University of Chicago.

Jonathan Glater and Alan Finder, "In Tuition Game, Popularity Rises with Price." ©December 12, 2006 by The New York Times.

Josie Glausiusz, "Seismologists Go Green." ©1999 by the Walt Disney Company.

Michael Pietrusewsky and Michele Toomay Douglas, "Intensification of Agriculture at Ban Chiang: Is There Evidence from the Skeletons?" ©2001 by University of Hawaii Press.

Karen Gust Schollmeyer and Christy G. Turner II, "Dental Caries, Prehistoric Diet, and the Pithouse-to-Pueblo Transition in Southwestern Colorado." ©2004 by Society for American Archaeology.

Wait for the supervisor's instructions before you open the page to the topic.
Please print and sign your name and write the date in the designated spaces below.

Time: 35 Minutes

General Directions

You will have 35 minutes in which to plan and write an essay on the topic inside. Read the topic and the accompanying directions carefully. You will probably find it best to spend a few minutes considering the topic and organizing your thoughts before you begin writing. In your essay, be sure to develop your ideas fully, leaving time, if possible, to review what you have written. **Do not write on a topic other than the one specified. Writing on a topic of your own choice is not acceptable.**

No special knowledge is required or expected for this writing exercise. Law schools are interested in the reasoning, clarity, organization, language usage, and writing mechanics displayed in your essay. How well you write is more important than how much you write.

Confine your essay to the blocked, lined area on the front and back of the separate Writing Sample Response Sheet. Only that area will be reproduced for law schools. Be sure that your writing is legible.

Both this topic sheet and your response sheet must be turned over to the testing staff before you leave the room.

Topic Code	Print Your Full Name Here		
	Last	First	M.I.

Date	Sign Your Name Here
/ /	

Scratch Paper
Do not write your essay in this space.

LSAT® Writing Sample Topic

Directions: The scenario presented below describes two choices, either one of which can be supported on the basis of the information given. Your essay should consider both choices and argue for one over the other, based on the two specified criteria and the facts provided. There is no "right" or "wrong" choice: a reasonable argument can be made for either.

The Wangs must arrange summer child care for their ten-year-old child. They have found two summer-long programs that are affordable and in which friends of their child would also be participating. Using the facts below, write an essay in which you argue for one program over the other based on the following two considerations:

- The Wangs want their child to enjoy activities that would add variety to the regular school experience.
- Transportation to the program must be easy for the Wangs to accommodate to their work situations.

City Summer is located at a college near Mrs. Wang's job but a considerable distance from Mr. Wang's. It offers early arrival and late pick-up times for parent convenience. Mrs. Wang has somewhat flexible work hours, but must travel overnight occasionally. City Summer offers classes in the visual arts, dance, drama, music, swimming, and gymnastics, as well as gym activities like basketball and volleyball. In addition, there are organized field trips to museums, plays, and historical sites. The program concludes with a presentation of student work from the classes.

Round Lake Camp is located 30 minutes outside the city. Bus transportation is provided to and from several city schools, one of which is next door to Mr. Wang's job. Pick-up and drop-off are at set times in the early morning and late afternoon. Mr. Wang has flexibility in his work starting time but often must work late. The camp has classes in swimming, sailing, archery, nature study, crafts, and outdoor skills. It also has regular free periods when campers can choose among outdoor activities or just explore the woods. At the end of the summer the campers have an overnight camping trip at a nearby state wilderness area.

WP-R095A

Scratch Paper
Do not write your essay in this space.

LAST NAME (Print)

L

FIRST NAME (Print)

LAST 4 DIGITS OF SOCIAL SECURITY/SOCIAL INSURANCE NO.

MI

TEST CENTER NO.

SIGNATURE

M M D D Y Y
TEST DATE

LSAC ACCOUNT NO.

TOPIC CODE

Writing Sample Response Sheet

DO NOT WRITE IN THIS SPACE

**Begin your essay in the lined area below.
Continue on the back if you need more space.**

COMPUTING YOUR SCORE

Directions:

1. Use the Answer Key on the next page to check your answers.

2. Use the Scoring Worksheet below to compute your raw score.

3. Use the Score Conversion Chart to convert your raw score into the 120-180 scale.

Scoring Worksheet

1. Enter the number of questions you answered correctly in each section.

	Number Correct
SECTION I	_____
SECTION II	_____
SECTION III	_____
SECTION IV..............	_____

2. Enter the sum here: _____

   This is your Raw Score.

Conversion Chart
For Converting Raw Score to the 120-180 LSAT Scaled Score
LSAT Form 0LSN85

Reported Score	Raw Score Lowest	Raw Score Highest
180	99	102
179	98	98
178	97	97
177	96	96
176	95	95
175	94	94
174	93	93
173	91	92
172	90	90
171	89	89
170	88	88
169	86	87
168	85	85
167	83	84
166	82	82
165	80	81
164	79	79
163	77	78
162	75	76
161	74	74
160	72	73
159	70	71
158	69	69
157	67	68
156	65	66
155	63	64
154	62	62
153	60	61
152	58	59
151	57	57
150	55	56
149	53	54
148	52	52
147	50	51
146	48	49
145	47	47
144	45	46
143	43	44
142	42	42
141	40	41
140	39	39
139	37	38
138	36	36
137	35	35
136	33	34
135	32	32
134	30	31
133	29	29
132	28	28
131	27	27
130	25	26
129	24	24
128	23	23
127	22	22
126	21	21
125	20	20
124	18	19
123	17	17
122	16	16
121	15	15
120	0	14

ANSWER KEY

SECTION I

1.	A	8.	D	15.	A	22.	D
2.	C	9.	A	16.	B	23.	C
3.	E	10.	E	17.	A	24.	B
4.	B	11.	E	18.	B	25.	E
5.	B	12.	D	19.	D	26.	E
6.	E	13.	C	20.	C	27.	C
7.	D	14.	B	21.	D		

SECTION II

1.	D	8.	A	15.	B	22.	D
2.	E	9.	C	16.	E	23.	C
3.	B	10.	B	17.	A	24.	E
4.	E	11.	A	18.	D	25.	A
5.	C	12.	E	19.	D	26.	E
6.	A	13.	D	20.	C		
7.	C	14.	B	21.	E		

SECTION III

1.	D	8.	C	15.	A	22.	A
2.	D	9.	B	16.	A	23.	D
3.	E	10.	B	17.	D		
4.	E	11.	A	18.	E		
5.	B	12.	C	19.	B		
6.	A	13.	E	20.	E		
7.	B	14.	C	21.	A		

SECTION IV

1.	C	8.	C	15.	D	22.	E
2.	D	9.	C	16.	B	23.	D
3.	A	10.	B	17.	D	24.	C
4.	C	11.	B	18.	D	25.	C
5.	B	12.	D	19.	B	26.	D
6.	A	13.	C	20.	E		
7.	C	14.	E	21.	A		

PREPTEST 63
JUNE 2011
FORM 2LSN93

SECTION I

Time—35 minutes

25 Questions

Directions: The questions in this section are based on the reasoning contained in brief statements or passages. For some questions, more than one of the choices could conceivably answer the question. However, you are to choose the best answer; that is, the response that most accurately and completely answers the question. You should not make assumptions that are by commonsense standards implausible, superfluous, or incompatible with the passage. After you have chosen the best answer, blacken the corresponding space on your answer sheet.

1. Backyard gardeners who want to increase the yields of their potato plants should try growing stinging nettles alongside the plants, since stinging nettles attract insects that kill a wide array of insect pests that damage potato plants. It is true that stinging nettles also attract aphids, and that many species of aphids are harmful to potato plants, but that fact in no way contradicts this recommendation, because _____.

Which one of the following most logically completes the argument?

(A) stinging nettles require little care and thus are easy to cultivate

(B) some types of aphids are attracted to stinging nettle plants but do not damage them

(C) the types of aphids that stinging nettles attract do not damage potato plants

(D) insect pests typically cause less damage to potato plants than other harmful organisms do

(E) most aphid species that are harmful to potato plants cause greater harm to other edible food plants

2. Jocko, a chimpanzee, was once given a large bunch of bananas by a zookeeper after the more dominant members of the chimpanzee's troop had wandered off. In his excitement, Jocko uttered some loud "food barks." The other chimpanzees returned and took the bananas away. The next day, Jocko was again found alone and was given a single banana. This time, however, he kept silent. The zookeeper concluded that Jocko's silence was a stratagem to keep the other chimpanzees from his food.

Which one of the following, if true, most seriously calls into question the zookeeper's conclusion?

(A) Chimpanzees utter food barks only when their favorite foods are available.

(B) Chimpanzees utter food barks only when they encounter a sizable quantity of food.

(C) Chimpanzees frequently take food from other chimpanzees merely to assert dominance.

(D) Even when they are alone, chimpanzees often make noises that appear to be signals to other chimpanzees.

(E) Bananas are a food for which all of the chimpanzees at the zoo show a decided preference.

3. A recent survey quizzed journalism students about the sorts of stories they themselves wished to read. A significant majority said they wanted to see stories dealing with serious governmental and political issues and had little tolerance for the present popularity of stories covering lifestyle trends and celebrity gossip. This indicates that today's trends in publishing are based on false assumptions about the interests of the public.

Which one of the following most accurately describes a flaw in the argument's reasoning?

(A) It takes what is more likely to be the effect of a phenomenon to be its cause.

(B) It regards the production of an effect as incontrovertible evidence of an intention to produce that effect.

(C) It relies on the opinions of a group unlikely to be representative of the group at issue in the conclusion.

(D) It employs language that unfairly represents those who are likely to reject the argument's conclusion.

(E) It treats a hypothesis as fact even though it is admittedly unsupported.

GO ON TO THE NEXT PAGE.

4. Electric bug zappers, which work by attracting insects to light, are a very effective means of ridding an area of flying insects. Despite this, most pest control experts now advise against their use, recommending instead such remedies as insect-eating birds or insecticide sprays.

Which one of the following, if true, most helps to account for the pest control experts' recommendation?

(A) Insect-eating birds will take up residence in any insect-rich area if they are provided with nesting boxes, food, and water.

(B) Bug zappers are less effective against mosquitoes, which are among the more harmful insects, than they are against other harmful insects.

(C) Bug zappers use more electricity but provide less light than do most standard outdoor light sources.

(D) Bug zappers kill many more beneficial insects and fewer harmful insects than do insect-eating birds and insecticide sprays.

(E) Developers of certain new insecticide sprays claim that their products contain no chemicals that are harmful to humans, birds, or pets.

5. Gardener: The design of Japanese gardens should display harmony with nature. Hence, rocks chosen for placement in such gardens should vary widely in appearance, since rocks found in nature also vary widely in appearance.

The gardener's argument depends on assuming which one of the following?

(A) The selection of rocks for placement in a Japanese garden should reflect every key value embodied in the design of Japanese gardens.

(B) In the selection of rocks for Japanese gardens, imitation of nature helps to achieve harmony with nature.

(C) The only criterion for selecting rocks for placement in a Japanese garden is the expression of harmony with nature.

(D) Expressing harmony with nature and being natural are the same thing.

(E) Each component of a genuine Japanese garden is varied.

6. Small experimental vacuum tubes can operate in heat that makes semiconductor components fail. Any component whose resistance to heat is greater than that of semiconductors would be preferable for use in digital circuits, but only if that component were also comparable to semiconductors in all other significant respects, such as maximum current capacity. However, vacuum tubes' maximum current capacity is presently not comparable to that of semiconductors.

If the statements above are true, which one of the following must also be true?

(A) Vacuum tubes are not now preferable to semiconductors for use in digital circuits.

(B) Once vacuum tubes and semiconductors have comparable maximum current capacity, vacuum tubes will be used in some digital circuits.

(C) The only reason that vacuum tubes are not now used in digital circuits is that vacuum tubes' maximum current capacity is too low.

(D) Semiconductors will always be preferable to vacuum tubes for use in many applications other than digital circuits.

(E) Resistance to heat is the only advantage that vacuum tubes have over semiconductors.

7. The cause of the epidemic that devastated Athens in 430 B.C. can finally be identified. Accounts of the epidemic mention the hiccups experienced by many victims, a symptom of no known disease except that caused by the recently discovered Ebola virus. Moreover, other symptoms of the disease caused by the Ebola virus are mentioned in the accounts of the Athenian epidemic.

Each of the following, if true, weakens the argument EXCEPT:

(A) Victims of the Ebola virus experience many symptoms that do not appear in any of the accounts of the Athenian epidemic.

(B) Not all of those who are victims of the Ebola virus are afflicted with hiccups.

(C) The Ebola virus's host animals did not live in Athens at the time of the Athenian epidemic.

(D) The Ebola virus is much more contagious than the disease that caused the Athenian epidemic was reported to have been.

(E) The epidemics known to have been caused by the Ebola virus are usually shorter-lived than was the Athenian epidemic.

GO ON TO THE NEXT PAGE.

8. Letter to the editor: Your article was unjustified in criticizing environmentalists for claiming that more wolves on Vancouver Island are killed by hunters than are born each year. You stated that this claim was disproven by recent studies that indicate that the total number of wolves on Vancouver Island has remained roughly constant for 20 years. But you failed to account for the fact that, fearing the extinction of this wolf population, environmentalists have been introducing new wolves into the Vancouver Island wolf population for 20 years.

Which one of the following most accurately expresses the conclusion of the argument in the letter to the editor?

(A) Environmentalists have been successfully maintaining the wolf population on Vancouver Island for 20 years.

(B) As many wolves on Vancouver Island are killed by hunters as are born each year.

(C) The population of wolves on Vancouver Island should be maintained by either reducing the number killed by hunters each year or introducing new wolves into the population.

(D) The recent studies indicating that the total number of wolves on Vancouver Island has remained roughly constant for 20 years were flawed.

(E) The stability in the size of the Vancouver Island wolf population does not warrant the article's criticism of the environmentalists' claim.

9. Computer scientist: For several decades, the number of transistors on new computer microchips, and hence the microchips' computing speed, has doubled about every 18 months. However, from the mid-1990s into the next decade, each such doubling in a microchip's computing speed was accompanied by a doubling in the cost of producing that microchip.

Which one of the following can be properly inferred from the computer scientist's statements?

(A) The only effective way to double the computing speed of computer microchips is to increase the number of transistors per microchip.

(B) From the mid-1990s into the next decade, there was little if any increase in the retail cost of computers as a result of the increased number of transistors on microchips.

(C) For the last several decades, computer engineers have focused on increasing the computing speed of computer microchips without making any attempt to control the cost of producing them.

(D) From the mid-1990s into the next decade, a doubling in the cost of fabricating new computer microchips accompanied each doubling in the number of transistors on those microchips.

(E) It is unlikely that engineers will ever be able to increase the computing speed of microchips without also increasing the cost of producing them.

GO ON TO THE NEXT PAGE.

10. Ms. Sandstrom's newspaper column describing a strange natural phenomenon on the Mendels' farm led many people to trespass on and extensively damage their property. Thus, Ms. Sandstrom should pay for this damage if, as the Mendels claim, she could have reasonably expected that the column would lead people to damage the Mendels' farm.

The argument's conclusion can be properly inferred if which one of the following is assumed?

(A) One should pay for any damage that one's action leads other people to cause if one could have reasonably expected that the action would lead other people to cause damage.

(B) One should pay for damage that one's action leads other people to cause only if, prior to the action, one expected that the action would lead other people to cause that damage.

(C) It is unlikely that the people who trespassed on and caused the damage to the Mendels' property would themselves pay for the damage they caused.

(D) Ms. Sandstrom knew that her column could incite trespassing that could result in damage to the Mendels' farm.

(E) The Mendels believe that Ms. Sandstrom is able to form reasonable expectations about the consequences of her actions.

11. Meyer was found by his employer to have committed scientific fraud by falsifying data. The University of Williamstown, from which Meyer held a PhD, validated this finding and subsequently investigated whether he had falsified data in his doctoral thesis, finding no evidence that he had. But the university decided to revoke Meyer's PhD anyway.

Which one of the following university policies most justifies the decision to revoke Meyer's PhD?

(A) Anyone who holds a PhD from the University of Williamstown and is found to have committed academic fraud in the course of pursuing that PhD will have the PhD revoked.

(B) No PhD program at the University of Williamstown will admit any applicant who has been determined to have committed any sort of academic fraud.

(C) Any University of Williamstown student who is found to have submitted falsified data as academic work will be dismissed from the university.

(D) Anyone who holds a PhD from the University of Williamstown and is found to have committed scientific fraud will have the PhD revoked.

(E) The University of Williamstown will not hire anyone who is under investigation for scientific fraud.

12. Aerobics instructor: Compared to many forms of exercise, kickboxing aerobics is highly risky. Overextending when kicking often leads to hip, knee, or lower-back injuries. Such overextension is very likely to occur when beginners try to match the high kicks of more skilled practitioners.

Which one of the following is most strongly supported by the aerobics instructor's statements?

(A) Skilled practitioners of kickboxing aerobics are unlikely to experience injuries from overextending while kicking.

(B) To reduce the risk of injuries, beginners at kickboxing aerobics should avoid trying to match the high kicks of more skilled practitioners.

(C) Beginners at kickboxing aerobics will not experience injuries if they avoid trying to match the high kicks of more skilled practitioners.

(D) Kickboxing aerobics is more risky than forms of aerobic exercise that do not involve high kicks.

(E) Most beginners at kickboxing aerobics experience injuries from trying to match the high kicks of more skilled practitioners.

13. A large company has been convicted of engaging in monopolistic practices. The penalty imposed on the company will probably have little if any effect on its behavior. Still, the trial was worthwhile, since it provided useful information about the company's practices. After all, this information has emboldened the company's direct competitors, alerted potential rivals, and forced the company to restrain its unfair behavior toward customers and competitors.

Which one of the following most accurately expresses the overall conclusion drawn in the argument?

(A) Even if the company had not been convicted of engaging in monopolistic practices, the trial probably would have had some effect on the company's behavior.

(B) The light shed on the company's practices by the trial has emboldened its competitors, alerted potential rivals, and forced the company to restrain its unfair behavior.

(C) The penalty imposed on the company will likely have little or no effect on its behavior.

(D) The company's trial on charges of engaging in monopolistic practices was worthwhile.

(E) The penalty imposed on the company in the trial should have been larger.

GO ON TO THE NEXT PAGE.

14. Waller: If there were really such a thing as extrasensory perception, it would generally be accepted by the public since anyone with extrasensory powers would be able to convince the general public of its existence by clearly demonstrating those powers. Indeed, anyone who was recognized to have such powers would achieve wealth and renown.

Chin: It's impossible to demonstrate anything to the satisfaction of all skeptics. So long as the cultural elite remains closed-minded to the possibility of extrasensory perception, the popular media reports, and thus public opinion, will always be biased in favor of such skeptics.

Waller's and Chin's statements commit them to disagreeing on whether

(A) extrasensory perception is a real phenomenon
(B) extrasensory perception, if it were a real phenomenon, could be demonstrated to the satisfaction of all skeptics
(C) skeptics about extrasensory perception have a weak case
(D) the failure of the general public to believe in extrasensory perception is good evidence against its existence
(E) the general public believes that extrasensory perception is a real phenomenon

15. Counselor: Hagerle sincerely apologized to the physician for lying to her. So Hagerle owes me a sincere apology as well, because Hagerle told the same lie to both of us.

Which one of the following principles, if valid, most helps to justify the counselor's reasoning?

(A) It is good to apologize for having done something wrong to a person if one is capable of doing so sincerely.
(B) If someone tells the same lie to two different people, then neither of those lied to is owed an apology unless both are.
(C) Someone is owed a sincere apology for having been lied to by a person if someone else has already received a sincere apology for the same lie from that same person.
(D) If one is capable of sincerely apologizing to someone for lying to them, then one owes that person such an apology.
(E) A person should not apologize to someone for telling a lie unless he or she can sincerely apologize to all others to whom the lie was told.

16. A survey of address changes filed with post offices and driver's license bureaus over the last ten years has established that households moving out of the city of Weston outnumbered households moving into the city two to one. Therefore, we can expect that next year's census, which counts all residents regardless of age, will show that the population of Weston has declined since the last census ten years ago.

Which one of the following, if true, most helps strengthen the argument?

(A) Within the past decade many people both moved into the city and also moved out of it.
(B) Over the past century any census of Weston showing a population loss was followed ten years later by a census showing a population gain.
(C) Many people moving into Weston failed to notify either the post office or the driver's license bureau that they had moved to the city.
(D) Most adults moving out of Weston were parents who had children living with them, whereas most adults remaining in or moving into the city were older people who lived alone.
(E) Most people moving out of Weston were young adults who were hoping to begin a career elsewhere, whereas most adults remaining in or moving into the city had long-standing jobs in the city.

17. Psychologist: People tend to make certain cognitive errors when they predict how a given event would affect their future happiness. But people should not necessarily try to rid themselves of this tendency. After all, in a visual context, lines that are actually parallel often appear to people as if they converge. If a surgeon offered to restructure your eyes and visual cortex so that parallel lines would no longer ever appear to converge, it would not be reasonable to take the surgeon up on the offer.

The psychologist's argument does which one of the following?

(A) attempts to refute a claim that a particular event is inevitable by establishing the possibility of an alternative event
(B) attempts to undermine a theory by calling into question an assumption on which the theory is based
(C) argues that an action might not be appropriate by suggesting that a corresponding action in an analogous situation is not appropriate
(D) argues that two situations are similar by establishing that the same action would be reasonable in each situation
(E) attempts to establish a generalization and then uses that generalization to argue against a particular action